D1348541

Castles and Colonists:
An archaeology of Elizabethan Ireland

18/8/17

Hi Sarah - meant to give you this yesterday, but forgot to put it in bag: it has temp? detail on all these places, but to benefit you need to be living in Ireland & able to plan a detour when visiting another uni, etc — so you seem the ideal reader.

P.

MANCHESTER
1824

Manchester University Press

The
Manchester
Spenser

The Manchester Spenser is a monograph and text series devoted to historical and textual approaches to Edmund Spenser – to his life, times, places, works and contemporaries.

A growing body of work in Spenser and Renaissance studies, fresh with confidence and curiosity and based on solid historical research, is being written in response to a general sense that our ability to interpret texts is becoming limited without the excavation of further knowledge. So the importance of research in nearby disciplines is quickly being recognised, and interest renewed: history, archaeology, religious or theological history, book history, translation, lexicography, commentary and glossary – these require treatment for and by students of Spenser.

The Manchester Spenser, to feed, foster and build on these refreshed attitudes, aims to publish reference tools, critical, historical, biographical and archaeological monographs on or related to Spenser, from several disciplines, and to publish editions of primary sources and classroom texts of a more wide-ranging scope.

The Manchester Spenser consists of work with stamina, high standards of scholarship and research, adroit handling of evidence, rigour of argument, exposition and documentation.

The series will encourage and assist research into, and develop the readership of, one of the richest and most complex writers of the early modern period.

General Editor J.B. Lethbridge
Editorial Board Helen Cooper, Thomas Herron, Carol V. Kaske,
James C. Nohrnberg & Brian Vickers

Also available

*Celebrating Mutabilitie: Essays on
Edmund Spenser's Mutabilitie Cantos* Jane Grogan (ed.)

Shakespeare and Spenser: Attractive opposites J.B. Lethbridge (ed.)

*Renaissance erotic romance: Philhellene Protestantism,
Renaissance translation and English literary politics* Victor Skretkowicz

Castles and Colonists

An archaeology of Elizabethan Ireland

ERIC KLINGELHOFER

Manchester University Press

Manchester and New York

distributed in the United States exclusively by Palgrave Macmillan

Published by Manchester University Press
Oxford Road, Manchester M13 9NR, UK
and Room 400, 175 Fifth Avenue, New York, NY 10010, USA
www.manchesteruniversitypress.co.uk

Distributed in the United States exclusively by
Palgrave Macmillan, 175 Fifth Avenue, New York,
NY 10010, USA

Distributed in Canada exclusively by
UBC Press, University of British Columbia, 2029 West Mall,
Vancouver, BC, Canada V6T 1Z2

British Library Cataloguing-in-Publication Data
A catalogue record for this book is available from the British Library

Library of Congress Cataloging-in-Publication Data applied for

ISBN   978 07190 8246 7   hardback

First published 2010

Typeset in Minion by
Koinonia, Manchester
Printed and Bound in Great Britain by
CPI Antony Rowe, Chippenham, Wiltshire

But that eternal fount of love and grace,
Still flowing forth his goodnesse unto all,
Now seeing left a waste and emptie place
In his wyde Pallace, through those Angels fall,
Cast to supply the same, and to enstall
A new unknowen Colony therein,
Whose root from earths base groundworke shold begin.

Edmund Spenser, *An Hymne of Heavenly Love*, 1596

Contents

List of figures

Unless otherwise indicated, all photos and drawings are by the author.

Acknowledgements

A long research project has many, many persons contributing to its success. I must first acknowledge my debt to those scholars who had previously studied similar aspects of Elizabethan Ireland and who generously shared with me the results of their research: David Quinn, Rolf Loeber, Paul Kerrigan, David Newman Johnson, and Con Manning. In Northern Ireland, Nick Brannon introduced me to Ulster Plantation sites, and in Cork, Mick Monk, a comrade from the trenches of Anglo-Saxon Southampton, welcomed my interest from the start. University College Cork, both the faculty and staff of his Department of Archaeology and John Irwin of the Civil Engineering Department, consistently provided material assistance to my fieldwork, and the Cork Archaeological Survey kindly shared their files with me. I am grateful to the members of both organizations, and also to Terry Barry and John Bradley, who encouraged my research and urged me to publish my conclusions. James Lyttleton has kindly kept me informed on contemporary fieldwork. Members of the International Spenser Society have opened my eyes to the world of *The Faerie Queene* and beyond; Sheila Cavanagh and Tom Herron have tactfully corrected my Spenserian errors. I am also grateful to reviewers for the Manchester Spenser series, who located infelicities in this text and brought to my attention recent publications.

Financial support for the Munster Plantation projects came from Mercer University, Earthwatch Institute, the National Committee on Archaeology of the Royal Irish Academy, and the Royal Archaeological Institute. Landowners who kindly permitted fieldwork were Colm Power at Dunboy Castle, the late Tom Leahy at Mogeely Castle, George and Ivy Tanner at Carrigeen, Patrick Higgins at Curraglass, and Charles Harold-Barry at Kilcolman Castle. Special thanks for help and hospitality go to Margaret Ridgway of Kilcolman Wildfowl Refuge, and to Arthur Montgomery and Anna Maria Hajbe of Doneraile Court. Eamon Horgan and the residents of Doneraile provided my teams much entertainment at the annual Faerie Queene Festival, as did the horse fairs at Mallow, Co. Waterford, and Buttevant, Co. Cork.

In the many seasons of fieldwork in Ireland, I had the good fortune to collaborate with a number of professional archaeologists and to be helped by many students, volunteers, and local enthusiasts. The Dunboy 1989 team comprised

Jada Hamby and Mark Hardin; the Mogeely 1990 team was Kieran Hoare and Roderick Klingelhofer; the Mogeely 1991 team comprised Alicia Bailey, Jennifer Neal, John Rawls, and Scott Turner. At Mogeely, Curraglass, and Carrigeen in 1992, Franc Myles co-directed, assisted by Peter Ball and Eamonn Cotter, with students Graham Austin, Ian Doyle, Caroline Sandes, John Skelton, and Bond Thomas. In 1993, with co-director Franc Myles, the staff comprised Peter Ball and Eamonn Cotter assisted by Aoife Christie, Ian Doyle, Alec Dundan, Ruth Kelly, Liz O'Driscoll, and Caroline Sandes, with volunteers Graham Austin, Marie Myhrman, Lotta Nyman, Laura Tallon, Angela Wallace, and Sharon Weadick.

At Kilcolman Castle, the 1993 staff comprised Eamonn Cotter, Bill Henry, Irene Henry, and Alexandra Klingelhofer; Team I was Joan Arbuthnot, Jim Brimhall, Karen Brimhall, Lee Davis, Mary Margaret Davis, Ruthanne Harstad, Pat Headley, Judy Lydon, Melody Settler, Kate Torgersen, Tom Tredway, and Pat Young; Team II was Irene Calero, Vicki Crouse, Bill Gould, and Tom Tredway; and Team III was Petra Beunderman, Sheila Cavanagh, Erik Clark, James Daugherty, Bob Harker, Ray Malafronte, Mary Beth Moriarty, Daniel Ranalli, Ben Shuford, Marlene Shuford, Susan Steele, Marcia Stone, and Robert Stone. The 1994 staff comprised Caroline Raison, Carter Hudgins, Jacinta Keiley, and Alexandra Klingelhofer; Team I was Joan Butterfield, David Clark, Maxine Clark, Jim Dunaway, Louise Dunaway, Rob Garcia, Kathy Irwin, Susie Phips, Jane Tonsula, and Jessica White; Team II was Cherie Blizzard, Ellen Drezka, Lauren Farber, John Fisher, Theresa Fisher, N. Ganesh, Ben Gettler, Melissa Gwynn, John Kelly, and Dean Koenig. The 1995 staff comprised Ian Doyle, Alycia Feindel, and Alexandra Klingelhofer; Team I was Christopher Davis, Anne Harvey, Michael Harvey, and Berit Huseby; Team II was Ese Burlingame, Pansy Collins, Wesley Cooper, John Croom, Roberta Darling, Theresa Donham, Cindy Jenkins, Wendy Long, Crysande Martin, Alton Sannar, Nancy Sanner, Charles Sides, Dan Thorpe, and Tanja Trivan. The 1996 staff members were Marie Blake, Wesley Cooper, Ian Doyle, Carter Hudgins, and Alexandra Klingelhofer; Team I was Wilma Bennett, Jane Campbell, Jennifer Dozio, Mary Gosline, Gary Harris, Patricia Harris, Ann Hearn, Beth Hearn, Dorothy Herzberg, Eva Kornreich, Janet Littlejohn, Maryann Ullman, Megan Weiss, Amy Wexler, and Jennifer Wexler; Team TT comprised Alan Barr, Alaistair Barr, Jack Konner, Emily Berlith, Richard Berlith, Maureen McAllister, and Ginny Ray.

Special thanks go to Eamonn Cotter and Clare McCutcheon, who guided me in the history and culture of County Cork, and to my American colleagues, Carter Hudgins and Bill and Irene Henry, who generously gave me their time and skills. My family had occasion to join me in County Cork, but for much of the decade they bore my summer absences with patience, for which I am grateful. I must thank above all my wife, Alexandra, a loving companion and wise adviser, both at home and abroad.

Introduction

To the Queene.
Out of the ashes of disolacon and wastnes of this your wretched realme of
Ireland. Vouchsafe moste mightie Empresse our Dred soveraigne to receive
the voices of a fewe moste unhappie Ghostes ... far from the light of your
gracious sunshine which spreadeth it selfe over Countries most remote ...
yet upon this miserable land being your owne just and heritable dominion
letteth no one little beam of your large mercie to be shed.
                                                    Edmund Spenser, 1598[1]

The epigraph offered at the beginning of this book reveals Spenser's image
of Man's creation as a divine plan to colonize that 'waste and emptie place'
forfeited by the Fallen Angels, a clear metaphor for Elizabeth's policy of
settling Ireland with English Protestants. Two years later, in the quote
above, he penned a desperate plea begging the Queen to help 'this miserable land'. No one spoke better for the colonial experience of Elizabeth's
Munster Plantation than a man who lived there throughout its existence,
who married and raised a family there, who served its government in
several positions, and who lost in its downfall all that he had gained.
Edmund Spenser, even more than Sir Walter Raleigh, who was by far the
largest landowner in Munster, wrote both directly and symbolically of
the land and the conditions of life there. Spenser had resurrected from
chivalric romances the idealized court and dreamland of *The Faerie
Queene*. As his prefatory letter to Raleigh explained, 'in my particular
I conceive the most excellent and glorious person of our soveraine the
Queene, and her kingdome in Faeryland'.[2] One could argue that Spenser,
by not limiting Faeryland specifically to England, may have considered
Ireland part of Elizabeth's 'kingdome [of] Faery land', perhaps as a distant
province. In any case, ten years after the meeting in Munster between
Raleigh and Spenser that led to the latter's visit to Elizabeth's court and
the printing of the first part of *The Faerie Queene*, Spenser's home, his

authority, and his dreams were 'ashes', and Ireland only a 'wretched realme'.

At the end of Elizabeth's reign the Munster settlement was indeed in ruins, a failure like all the other colonial 'plantings' or 'plantations' of English people overseas. This book examines how this occurred, and what material evidence survives for the short-lived colony.[3] It is an archaeology of Elizabethan Ireland, that is, the Ireland that Elizabethan Englishmen and women created, albeit limitedly and briefly. For the Irish, this period marks the renewal of a series of forced changes in government, landowning, and culture by which Irishness was replaced by institutions and behaviour approved of, and even dictated by, London. But because the English attempted several colonies scattered over different continents during the last half of Elizabeth's reign, this book must also consider activities in Ireland within the context of nascent efforts to establish an Elizabethan Empire. Documentary evidence for these developments having been thoroughly plumbed, another avenue of research, the archaeology of the proto-colonial period, can help bring new information to the matter.

A personal motive for undertaking the archaeology of the Munster Plantation was the realization of its potential value, when my excavation of early colonial sites in Virginia during the 1970s led me to consider their precedents. The later colonies of Ulster and Massachusetts have been the standard locations for comparative material, both documentary and archaeological. Yet, by the fact that it preceded Jamestown by twenty years, the Tudor colony in southern Ireland was to me logically more relevant to the early settlement of Virginia (as well as Bermuda and Newfoundland) than were the Ulster and Massachusetts colonies. And as the only even partially successful Tudor colonizer in the New World, Sir Walter Raleigh's lordships in Munster provide evidence directly comparable to his contemporary colonial site at Roanoke, North Carolina, and his outposts in the Caribbean, which I am currently investigating. Thus, Elizabethan Ireland, and especially the Munster Plantation, can be the key to understanding the archaeology of the Elizabethan Empire and the more permanent Atlantic colonial settlements that followed it. Munster reveals the weakness of the Tudor state in marshalling its resources in Ireland, despite the dominance of English arms, governance, and economic productivity. Fatally underestimating Irish resistance, a colonial attitude of ethnic and cultural superiority was expressed on the ground by woefully unprepared security forces, the landholders' reluctance to remove native populations, and an architecture having the appearance of strength, but erected without mortar bonding.

Proto-colonial archaeology, studying the first generations of European expansion, is a restricted field, focusing on a few places over a few centuries. Yet it concerns a topic of great importance: the physical origins of the world culture that now surrounds us, derived from the descendants of European settlers and those they ruled. These sites show how the English and others first responded to the challenges of new environments and new peoples, and how their choices led to conquest, adaption, or failure. Archaeologists seek to discover, understand, and preserve if possible, before they are lost forever, the rare traces of these earliest European outposts, both firstborn and stillborn. The Empire of Elizabeth, in Ireland and elsewhere, belongs to the latter.

Given the limited research undertaken so far, this book cannot fully satisfy the rising demands for information on southern Ireland's Plantation Period, Elizabethan material culture, or the personal lives of Edmund Spenser and other Renaissance figures. It is intended, rather, to present my views on the topic to a knowledgeable audience in Ireland and Britain, while informing the wider, literary-based readership of the Manchester Spenser series. A better book, I'm sure, could be written in twenty years' time and with a more thorough use of historical sources, especially estate papers, but that would mean postponing it for another generation. Wishing to add to current scholarship, but waiting until my excavation reports were published, I have assembled the findings of my research projects in County Cork and the conclusions that I have drawn from them. The resulting book is not as comprehensive or cohesive a rendering of the past as I would wish, which is why it is titled a contributory *An Archaeology*, not a definitive *The Archaeology*. The latter would be a superior work, but I do not believe it can be written yet, nor should it be attempted. The field of archaeology is littered enough with the husks of premature publication.

Notes

1 *A briefe note of Ireland*, R. Gottfried (ed.), *Spenser's Prose Works* (Baltimore, 1946) p. 236.

2 'A letter of the authors', F. M. Padelford (ed.), *The Faerie Queene Book One* (Baltimore, 1932), p. 168.

3 Portions of this work have been drawn from the results of research projects published from 1992 to 2005. I am grateful for permission to use material from the following: 'The Renaissance fortifications at Dunboy Castle, 1602: a report on the 1989 excavations', *J. Cork Hist. and Archaeol. Soc.* 97 (1992), pp. 85–96; 'Castles Built with Air: Spenserian architecture in Ireland', in *Military Studies in Medieval Europe: Papers of the 'Medieval Europe Brugge 1997' Conference*, vol. 11, Guy de Boe and Frans Verhaeghe (eds),

Instituut voor het Archeologisch Patrimonium (Zellik, Belgium, 1997), pp. 149–54; 'Proto-colonial archaeology: the case of Elizabethan Ireland', in P. Funari, M. Hall, and S. Jones (eds), *Back from the Edge: Archaeology in History*, One World Archaeology series (London, 1999) pp. 164–79; 'The castle of the *Faerie Queene*', *Archaeology*, March/April (1999), pp. 48–52; 'Elizabethan settlements at Mogeely Castle, Curraglass and Carrigeen, Co. Cork (Part I)', *J. Cork Hist. and Archaeol. Soc.*, 104 (1999), pp. 97–110; 'Elizabethan settlements at Mogeely Castle, Curraglass and Carrigeen, Co. Cork Part II', *J. Cork Hist. and Archaeol. Soc.*, 105 (2000), pp. 155–74; 'The architecture of empire: Elizabethan country houses in Ireland', pp. 102–15 in Susan Lawrence (ed.), *The Archaeologies of the British* (London, 2003); and 'Edmund Spenser at Kilcolman Castle: the archaeological evidence', *Post-Medieval Archaeol.* 39 No. 1 (2005), pp. 133–54.

1

Archaeology and Elizabeth's empire

The marvelous Priviledge of Brytish Impire ... wealth and strength, foreign
love and feare, and triumphant fame, the whole world over.

John Dee, 1577[1]

This chapter examines the role of archaeology in the study of the Elizabethan colonization of southern Ireland. Initial foreign settlement by early
modern European states, or by their authorized commercial organizations, are usefully characterized as the 'proto-colonial phase' of the epoch
of modern colonial imperialism. For European overseas activities, the
proto-colonial period may be generalized as c. 1450–1650. The 'planting'
of English colonists in the late sixteenth and early seventeenth centuries
is recognized as an important step in English colonialism and a turning
point in Irish history, but twentieth-century politics and policies discouraged its study.[2] The colonist in Irish nationalist history was no more than
a 'predatory Protestant'.[3] After recent revisionist work by historians,
however, such publications as *The Illustrated Archaeology of Ireland* have
recognized the significance of the proto-colonial or 'Plantation' period,
and archaeological research on the Munster colony in the Irish Republic
has followed the initiative of work undertaken on the Ulster colony in
Northern Ireland.[4]

Proto-colonial activities

The context of colonization

Elizabethan colonization is often viewed as something outside of – separate from – the overall course of European expansion. On the east side
of the Atlantic, it was once seen as an expression of the British Empire
to come, implicitly a civilizing force bringing the benefits of English
language, laws, and common decency. Looking at the domestic conflicts
of the Stuart period, an alternate view held that Elizabeth's overseas enter-

prises were spawned by a militant Protestantism defending England from a global Catholic conspiracy. On the west side of the Atlantic, colonization was believed to have stemmed from an ideological conflict between absolutism and democracy, as current assumptions about the political ideals of Pilgrim and Puritan 'fathers' were projected onto an earlier, Elizabethan generation.[5]

Late twentieth-century scholarship asserts that the motives and methods leading to early English colonies differed little from the forces behind French, Dutch, Spanish, or even Swedish colonization. European power was expanding, and at the same time its constituent parts, nation states and dynastic states, were in constant competition within Europe and overseas.[6] Colonies, even more than commercial ventures, were strategic responses to perceived threats. They were part of the chess game of dynastic and proto-nationalistic competition. Like war to von Clausewitz, colonization was an extension of politics in Machiavellian late Renaissance. But poorly developed economies, a rudimentary state apparatus, and the non-stop competition among nations meant that colonization was haphazardly implemented, even when a firm policy was formulated. Limited resources led to a constant juggling of priorities.

For Tudor England, one can make three observations. First, colonization was pragmatic and was often proposed as an opportunistic response to new conditions. Voyages of discovery, new economic directions, and international politics, all could stimulate colonial ventures. Religious proselytization was often touted as a reason to colonize, but the Church establishment had little real involvement in overseas expansion. Second, all Tudor colonial enterprises were related to some degree. There may have been differences in distances involved and the types of colonization, but not among decision-making and patronage groups. These comprised the Court, military adventurers, and the commercial investors of London and other major ports, in varying combinations. Third, military considerations always played a role in colonization, if only for the immediate defence of the settlers, but often at a strategic level. As such, colonizing voyages should be considered moves in an imperial strategy, and the colonies themselves as part of an Elizabethan Empire. This proto-colonial polity was of course ephemeral, existing in theory and on paper – and occasionally in fact – as colonies appeared and disappeared. Yet the efforts to establish an English overseas empire were no less real than those that led to the British Empire. John Dee's quote (above) assumes England's control of Ireland and domination of Scotland as the basis for a globally expanding 'Brytish Impire'.

The great achievement of Elizabeth's reign was in maintaining the status quo regarding England's possessions and security; it projected English power only momentarily. Her failure to reclaim Calais under the terms of the treaty of Cateau-Cambrésis was perhaps balanced by English control for twenty years of the three Dutch 'cautionary towns' of Flushing, Brill, and Ramekins. Her expansion of the navy and its use by the Sea Hawks to attack Spanish shipping and seaports compelled Philip to divert imperial resources in costly defensive measures. In this strategic competition, colonizing enterprises in the Arctic, Ireland, Newfoundland, Virginia, and Guiana were pieces in an essentially defensive game on the part of the queen. Certainly that is how James I acted when he permitted Raleigh to go to Guiana under such conditions that the king would succeed either by Raleigh's acquiring for England a gold-rich territory without challenging Spain, or by his failure and execution, and the consequently improved relations with Spain. In the game of empire, a colony was as much a chess-piece as Raleigh.

The security achieved in Elizabeth's reign, and in that of her successor James, created a new level of commercial activity and new organizations for capital formation, the chartered joint stock companies. E. P. Cheney went so far as to claim that 'the whole advance of English discovery, commerce, and colonization in the sixteenth and seventeenth centuries was due not to individuals but to the efforts of corporate bodies.'[7] The Crown and the City enjoyed a symbiotic relationship; the government received revenue from granting charters, as well as enhanced power in its ability to reward its friends, and the business community received protected monopolies and, less often, direct royal investment in cash or shipping. Ireland, however, was halfway between a home market and a colonial-commercial venture. Cheney noted the close relationship between the personalities involved in Ireland and the overseas commerce and colonization, like Thomas Smith and Walter Raleigh. Furthermore, schemes for groups or 'consorts' of investors to carry out settlement in Elizabethan Ireland presaged the later 'company' colonies in Virginia, Bermuda, and Ulster.

One must recognize, then, that for the English Crown, transatlantic colonization was not the colonialism of later political philosophies, but one of many diplomatic, military, and commercial tools. Cisatlantic colonization – in Ireland – was one option among other policies to protect England by controlling the archipelago. Although the successful Jacobean planting of the northern province of Ulster was and still is a most important element in the history of the British Isles, there were several previous colonial attempts in Ireland, the greatest of which concerned Munster province in the southwest of the island.

The collapse of the Munster colony in 1598, and the ensuing years of hard conquest by Elizabeth's generals, was due to the same errors of policy and perception that in the twentieth century would lead to a widespread rejection of English rule. Nevertheless, despite support from the Crown that was changeable at best and financial backing from commercial sources that demanded quick returns from investments, colonies in Munster and Carolina, Baffin Island and Trinidad did materialize. These serious attempts were physically undertaken, while places like Newfoundland and California were briefly visited and witnessed only the flourish of flag and drum. The universal failure or 'loss' of Elizabethan colonies was largely due to grossly inadequate supplies. This in turn was caused by insufficient knowledge of the localities and their inhabitants. Perhaps even more importantly, English understanding of colonization itself was poor. From lack of national experience, they sought guidance from Classical sources, Renaissance writings, and the real presence of the Spanish Empire.

Evidence for Elizabethan colonization exists: archival, pictorial, and physical. The archival survives in the written form of documents, charters, reports, and letters. Scholars such as David Quinn and Nicholas Canny have diligently sifted through the material; rarely do new items come to light. Pictorial evidence survives as a handful of drawings of colonial activities and a larger number of maps and picture maps, often in the form of prints accompanying published accounts. Again, this material has been widely published, though some individual maps may still be unrecognized or not well understood. It is the physical evidence – the standing, preserved, and buried structures and objects associated with the Elizabethan colonization – that has thus far been little touched and offers the most rewarding avenue for future research. To address Elizabethan colonial imperialism in Ireland, one must first consider its contemporary activities across the Atlantic.

America

Outside Europe, Englishmen sought and sometimes received Elizabeth's backing in planting colonies from the Arctic to the Equator. If successful, they would have presaged by more than a century the British Empire's domination of North America and effective presence in the Caribbean. It would have been a powerful counter-balance to Philip's Latin America colossus. But her transatlantic empire failed to materialize; not one of her colonies succeeded. If one cannot claim that Elizabeth created them as mere pawns in her great Hapsburg war, to be sacrificed for the greater security of England, neither should one claim some overarching plan of westward colonization; all evidence indicates that each effort was opportunistic and grew out of earlier discoveries and immediate expectations.

Martin Frobisher returned in 1578 to the edge of the Arctic, to Baffin Island, which he believed was at the entrance to a North-West Passage from the Atlantic to Asia. Contemporary voyages eastward into the Russian Arctic had found a tenuous trade route south to Moscow, but little opportunity to advance further into Siberia. Members of the Muscovy Company backed Frobisher's expeditions and were pleased to hear of the likely passage to the Orient, but were overwhelmed by the reported discovery of untouched gold deposits. The third expedition, well funded by the public, planned to exploit this ore and set up a permanent colony at the site, a frigid rock named Countess of Warwick Island, now known by its Inuit name, Kodlunarn. Despite careful planning, the expedition faced the real problems of survival in the far north. Terrifying storms scattered the fleet, sending supplies and prefabricated housing to the bottom of the sea. The sparse native population proved hostile, and the island's only fortification comprised a trench and bank across the neck of a small, cliff-faced promontory. Unsurprisingly, many questioned the plan to stay over the winter. Though some of the hundred soldiers and miners did volunteer, thinking of the riches they would be sitting on, it is to the credit of the otherwise rash commander that he refused to leave these the men to an obvious doom. One building was constructed, out of local stone and mortar, as an experiment to see how it would survive a winter. But the English never returned to find out. The tons of rocks they mined under such hardships proved to be iron pyrites – fool's gold. The project yielded no return at all for the investment, and Elizabeth jailed the leaders for what the public assumed was a vast swindle.[8]

In the mid-nineteenth century the American explorer Charles Francis Hall found Frobisher's site, and in the late twentieth century, fieldwork by Canadian and US teams corroborated his findings.[9] The foundations of the colonists' house remained, the Inuits having removed the items left within and others presumably buried outside. Some pieces of sea-coal and fragments of Renaissance stove tile indicated how it had been heated in a land without wood. One area was identified as a forge, another as a cutting or slip for boat repair. Swept by arctic winds, Frobisher's site remains a testament to the Elizabethans' exploits and to their folly.

Undeterred, other Englishmen dreamed of settling new territories on the far Atlantic shore. The explorer John Cabot had named Newfoundland, and claimed it for England, under Elizabeth's grandfather, Henry VII. Promising to take up this claim and advance it with mainland colonies was Sir Humphrey Gilbert, one of the early adventurers to Ireland, who convinced Elizabeth in 1578 of the value of fishing and furs, and the possibility of a temperate passage through North America. Gilbert planted the flag of St George on Newfoundland in 1583 and was acknowledged as the legitimate authority by astonished fishermen of assorted nationalities who used the coves there to dry their catch each summer. Unimpressed by what he had seen there, Gilbert sailed off to plant his colony, probably in the region of New England. His ship disappeared in a storm, and he became a national hero.[10]

Gilbert never colonized, but he left behind his plans and his royal charter, which his brother, Sir Walter Raleigh, quickly took up. Raleigh, by now the Queen's favorite, was forbidden to go himself. Nevertheless, he sent several expeditions to the mid-Atlantic coast to establish a colony that could maintain itself through local resources and serve as a base for privateers against Spain. The first group of colonists was brought to Roanoke Island, North Carolina, by Sir Richard Grenville in 1585. On the way there, he stopped in Puerto Rico to refit and gather supplies, erecting a fortified camp that he used to taunt the Spanish government. Despite the possibility that he might want to make the English foothold permanent and enlarge it by conquest, much of his fleet had already gone to the North Carolina rendezvous, so he moved on from this first English site in the Caribbean. John White, Raleigh's artist, drew a picture map of the fort, which topographical study has used to identify the site's location. Remote sensing techniques and limited archaeological testing have yielded tantalizing data, but for Grenville's fortification, the evidence is suggestive at best.[11]

This is not the case on Roanoke Island. There, eighteenth-century maps actually marked a spot as Raleigh's Fort, later Fort Raleigh. This survived as low earthworks, visited by many, including US Presidents Monroe and Roosevelt, until the National Park Service excavated and restored them in the 1950s. Barely sixty feet across, the small defences comprised a rough square, with large projecting bastions on the three sides, the fourth containing an opening. The fieldwork has been identified as a 'sconce', much used in the contemporary Dutch wars. It would have mounted cannon that the Roanoke colonists were known to have brought with them. The records also refer to a town nearby, with a number of wooden houses. No evidence has yet been found for the residences of this first English settlement in the New World. The colony was essentially a military one; its governor was Captain Ralph Lane, whose leadership kept the English busy and reasonably effective, it seems, but whose demands upon local Indian food supplies soon grew intolerable and were resisted. An important member of the expedition was Thomas Harriot, a scientist in the employ of Raleigh, whose observations on the geography, natural resources, and native inhabitants became the foundation for studying the continent. In the early 1990s archaeologists were able to identify, close to the fort, the location of Harriot's workshop. In this wooden structure, a metallurgist from Prague tested ore for precious metals using a brick furnace and crucibles. Other samples were collected and studied in European ceramic and glass vessels. Not far was a pit for making charcoal for the furnace, and some evidence for brick production. The next summer Lane's colony was withdrawn, and a small occupying part of English soldiers was soon driven off the island to an unknown fate.[12]

Raleigh meanwhile changed the structure of the colony, replacing seigneurial authority with a corporate and commercial organization. The new colonists, with John White as governor, were led by men who had a stake in the enterprise, and together planned to found the City of Raleigh in the newly named Virginia. This was the famous Lost Colony of 1587, which was unable to establish a new settlement, and reoccupied the town and fort on Roanoke. White soon left for England to resupply the colony, but his return was delayed for two years by the Spanish Armada. When he finally reached Roanoke, the only sign he found of his family and friends was the name 'Croatoan' carved on the fort's gatepost (and partially repeated on a tree by the shore), indicating that the group had moved to the safety of a friendly tribe by that name, further out on the barrier islands. No one knows if they ever reached Croatoan safely, though theories abound.

Raleigh clung to the hope that his colony survived, if only to retain the charter that gave him sole access to North America. Nevertheless, it was South America that drew him next. Following up the Spanish stories of El Dorado that his employees had heard, Raleigh finally got Elizabeth's permission to sail to America, and in 1595 he set off in search of the City of Gold, the expected third New World civilization of great wealth. He believed he was arriving just in time to prevent the Spanish governor of the just-settled Trinidad from mounting an expedition up the Orinoco to claim the prize. Raleigh initiated his conquests for Elizabeth with a swift assault on Trinidad, driving out the Spanish and liberating local Indians who had been treated cruelly. He was eager to explore Guiana and locate El Dorado, but first fortified a position on Trinidad that would protect his fleet from any Spanish counterattack. Mounting several cannon, this fort was well constructed of earthworks and timber. Yet it was never attacked. Instead of being the key defence of a tropical Elizabethan empire, it and Trinidad were soon abandoned by Sir Walter Raleigh, whose discoveries had produced only fever, hunger, and valueless ore samples. For years, the natives of the region believed that Raleigh would return and deliver them from the Spanish. Yet the account he published fails to mention the abandoned fort, and it is from Spanish documents that one learns of this short-term threat to the Spanish Caribbean. The descriptions permit the fort site to be identified at Los Gallos Point, and like Grenville's fort on Puerto Rico, it has recently been the object of archaeological search.[13]

And like the 1585 fort site on Puerto Rico, the 1595 fort site from the expedition to El Dorado has not yet produced definitive archaeological data. Raleigh did return to the area, some twenty years later, but it was a tragic attempt to elude the traitor's fate that King James had ordered for him. By that time, English expansion had really begun. Ulster was planted with Protestants, Jamestown and scores of other Virginia settlements had taken root, and Bermuda was already counted as the second transatlantic colony of a post-Elizabethan empire. Yet these successful Jacobean enterprises, and indeed the seventeenth-century foundation of the English (British) Empire, were elements of a long development that began with ill-fated Elizabethan colonial settlements.

Proto-colonial Ireland (see Figure 1.1)

The late medieval Irish economy was largely a self-sustaining agriculture, with arable dominant in a few Anglicized areas, and pastoral dominant elsewhere. In the Tudor period, most rural exchange of goods and wealth still flowed through the tribute due to lordship and the generosity expected of it, not to markets.[14] Urban centres were few outside the walled port towns that supplied specialized and luxury items. Cloth had always been the most important trade for medieval Europe, and the Irish had participated in a large linen trade with England until the early sixteenth century, when the demand for finished cloth was replaced by one for yarn. Woollen cloth was also produced, but only the famous Irish rug or mantle remained a popular export. As part of the Atlantic trade to Spain and Italy, the monopolistic port towns prospered to the detriment

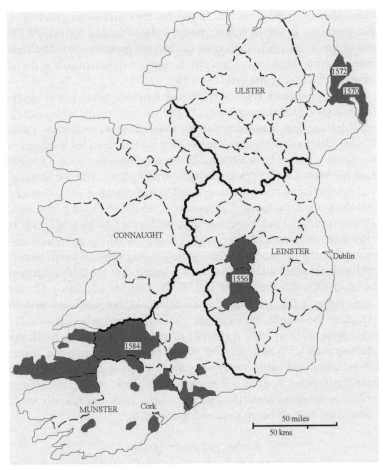

Figure 1.1 Elizabethan Ireland. County boundaries are those of 1603. Shaded areas are lands settled by the English under Mary and Elizabeth.

of the rural Irish, exchanging sheepskins, furs, and decreasing cloth but increasing hides and timber, for wine, salt, and iron.[15]

In the early modern period, more detailed information is available. Local records suggest that sheep rearing was more important in Munster than in the rest of Ireland.[16] The port books of English cities and the records of the English and Irish councils indicate that the early sixteenth century saw imports of wood, hops, and beer from southeast England. This later shifted to wheat, malt, and beans from eastern England, salt from Lancashire, and other field crops from the West Country via Bristol. The Irish sent in return butter, cheese, hides, fish, and textiles. At the end of the century, the shifting of the herring grounds weakened Irish fisheries, while there was an increase in timber exports, mainly as barrel staves for the fishing and wine industries.[17]

In the seventeenth century, trade took new directions, but in uncertain markets. English grain prices finally fell after rising for a century, which meant that Irish commodities would have more relative value. Timber exports continued to rise until the deforestation led to concerns for future supplies. Irish cattle made dramatic inroads into the English markets. West Country graziers bought so many Irish cattle for fattening that English cattle breeders complained to Parliament in 1621, claiming that the market was flooded by an incredible 100,000 head per annum. This in itself may reveal a specialization within the English cattle trade as some areas concentrated on rearing instead of breeding, and it may also reflect the new demand for meat by the growing regional towns associated with the cloth and coal industries. In any case the Irish cattlemen found markets that the English and Welsh could not adequately fill. The textile industry, however, was in a state of flux. A three-fold boom in cloth exports of the New Draperies for the Mediterranean market followed the peace with Spain in 1604. As part of Bristol-based triangular trade, the Munster ports of Waterford, Cork, and Limerick exported grain, frieze, tallow, hides, and barrel staves to Spain. Irish cloth producers seem to have participated both as sub-market contributors to English exports and as competitors when the cheaper, coarser Irish and Spanish wools brought the English boom to an end in the 1620s.[18]

Earlier Tudor colonization

Henry VIII may be said to have initiated early modern Irish history, when on 18 July 1541 he was proclaimed King – instead of Lord – of Ireland. Thus Ireland became a kingdom from the top down, and the Tudors found themselves committed to 'nation-building' both at home and abroad. England was then barely a Renaissance society, but the social and political dynamics of the rural Irish remained medieval in character: the clan was the primary secular institution, and real power lay with the many local lords who rarely ruled more than the land they could see from the tops of ubiquitous small 'tower-house' castles. In the late twelfth century, lords and knights of Norman origin had left England for power and position in Ireland, but for the last two centuries their ties to England had weakened as inter-marriage with the Irish clan nobility affected their cultural affiliation. Henry VIII moved to redress this dangerous trend by a policy of Anglicization, the slow – and ultimately incomplete – process of replacing Irish political culture and institutions with English ones. He created earls out of Irish clan chiefs and, by the policy of 'surrender and regrant', tried to convert traditional Irish landholding into English tenure by royal charter.

When Henry died in 1547, however, the lack of firm royal control in Ireland required further action. The initial step in the proto-colonial process was a military one. As Lord Protector in Edward VI's minority reign, the Duke of Somerset expanded the defence of The Pale, the English-controlled Dublin region, by a chain of military outposts similar to the English enclave around Calais on the French coast.[19]

The Tudor dynasty moved to secure both of these remnants of England's medieval empire. Calais was lost to France before plans for Renaissance artillery fortification and new colonial settlement there were realized. Ireland thus became England's only permanent overseas possession (excepting the Channel Isles) until the 1607 foundation of Jamestown,

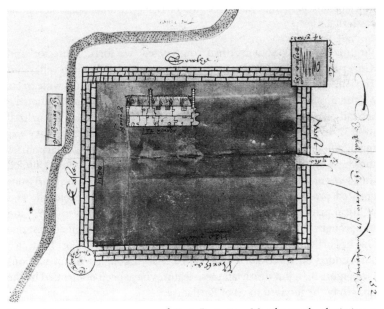

Figure 1.2 Contemporary map of Fort Protector, Maryborough, depicting a rectangular enclosure with opposing corner defences comprising a round bastion and a rectangular tower, and garrison buildings.

Figure 1.3 A corner of the circuit wall and rampart of Fort Governor, Philipstown. Standing remains indicate a rectangular enclosure lacking bastions, but with opposed projecting gates. The stub of Daingean tower-house lies in the centre of the fort.

Virginia. By 1548, Somerset had constructed two forts, 'Protector' and 'Governor', to control the low watershed between the Shannon valley and The Pale (see Figures 1.2, 1.3). The two garrisons were allotted wide tracts of land around the forts. Edward's sister and successor, Mary, initiated a second phase, planting English settlers in the areas that were formalized in 1557 as Queen's County (Laois) and King's County (Offaly). Mary was much influenced by her husband, Philip of Spain, and his colonial policies may have served as a model for the English government when it founded the towns of Maryborough and Philipstown at the forts.[20] Royal garrisons ensured prosperity for the settlements, which received economic and political privileges when changing status to market towns in 1567, and to boroughs in 1569.[21] Philipstown seems to have been built against one side of Fort Governor while a late Elizabethan map shows Fort Protector surrounded on three sides by a walled Maryborough without bastions (see Figure 3.3), but nearly all these features have been obliterated by the growth of the modern town of Portlaoise.[22]

Elizabethan colonization

Elizabeth repeatedly altered her policy on Ireland, as she vacillated between advice to ensure a united realm by placating the Irish and counsel to repress all rebellion and keep Ireland loyal by filling it with English people. Colonization evolved in stages, by decades, with increasing scale and success. Elizabeth received many petitions for specific colonizing ventures in Ireland and sometimes accepted them. In the late 1560s, a West Country group supported by Robert Dudley, Earl of Leicester, began colonial projects in the Munster province of southwest Ireland. Warham St Leger brought settlers to Kerricurrihy manor near Cork, which the Irish soon resisted, destroying the colony. Another proposed venture was public, with a corporate body and attracting merchant investment by acquiring monopolies. This overly ambitious group wanted to settle the south coast of Munster, and defend it for the queen, if she would grant them title to the coastal land along with complete fishing rights. Elizabeth rejected the request, but the Kerrycurrihy colony was revived, and served as the model for later English settlement in Munster.[23]

Both Sir Thomas Smith and Walter Devereux, the Earl of Essex, tried and failed in the early 1570s to establish colonies in the Ulster province of northeast Ireland.[24] Smith and his namesake son wrote broadsheets to attract participation in their scheme, appealing for subscriptions, which would serve as joint shares in the enterprise. They proposed to build a city, 'Elizabetha', surrounded by English-style villages with parish churches and landholdings of 300 acres to be worked by servile Irish 'churls'.[25] Arable production was the goal, first to the Irish market, then to England, France, and Spain. Smith's attempt to use a joint-stock company for colonization failed due to the short-term profit interests of most of the investors and to the lack of royal involvement, especially militarily.[26] The Earl of Essex brought over a large force, which was wasted by lengthy campaigns against a mobile enemy instead of defending newly established communities in zones purged of rebels. Landowning and the profits from farming rents were to be the attraction for participants in his colony.

Soon after Mary's brief reign, then, private attempts at Irish colonization took place, but the difficulty in raising capital and colonists and the political uncertainties of Elizabeth's early years on the throne prevented any long-term success. Yet the increasing strength of Elizabeth's government provided a new opportunity for expansion into Ireland. In open rebellion from 1579 to his death in 1583, the Earl of Desmond, the greatest lord and largest landowner in the province of Munster, led his generation's resistance to the Tudor monarchy in Dublin. Desmond tried to transform a feudal squabble into a national and religious cause, but ultimately ensured his destruction and that of his family by allying with the Jesuits and the Spanish, who were mortal threats to the now-Protestant Tudor regime. Elizabeth, exasperated by yet another important Irish lord rebelling against her government in Dublin, but alarmed by the Papal expeditionary force that had tried to spark an anti-Protestant revolt, in 1582 began to confiscate the Desmond lands. Most of these scattered estates were held by his clients or vassals, but the Crown claimed all under the law of treason, and they totaled about one fourth of the entire province. Beset by clamorous courtiers, Elizabeth took the momentous decision to regrant the land not to Irish claimants, but to Englishmen who would bring to the province thousands of settlers of unquestioned loyalty, a not insignificant point given international Catholic opposition to her rule. In 1586, surveying parties began to record the escheated lands for the new grantees, and the colony was born.[27]

Munster thus became a quasi-colony, described as a 'plantation', with one fourth of the province under new owners, but the remainder in local hands. The grantees of the 12,000-acre 'seignories' were figures at Court or those connected to London merchant guilds, but several thousand English settlers found little welcome from the displaced Irish population. Success in Munster would have brought about an area secure for Elizabeth, from which her power could spread to encompass the island. But when the rebel Earl of Tyrone's forces marched south from Ulster in October 1598, they met little effective resistance. The Munster colony collapsed. Refugees streamed into the walled cities, and within a few weeks the English held only four places outside those walls. Over the next five years, Elizabeth was forced to raise more than one new army and try out several commanders before Lord Mountjoy ended all resistance just as the queen lay dying in 1603.

Ambitious plans had soon appeared for the new colonial settlements. A proposal made in 1585 for Munster contained a scheme to establish hundreds to replicate the judicial and taxing divisions of an English county/shire, each of which would contain nearly 1000 families.[28] In what must have been a great disappointment to the grantees, migration to Munster may have reached only one-tenth that amount.[29] The tracts of escheated Desmond lands were widely scattered, and the native population refused to assist the surveying of the expropriated lands. And where holdings were established, the new grants were contested by Irish claimants to lands not personally owned by the Earl of Desmond. The grantees were rarely able to replace completely the Irish inhabitants with English farmers and artisans. Yet the Munster estates badly needed workers; it is estimated that perhaps one-third of the population there had died, most from the scorched earth policy employed to suppress the Desmond rebellion.[30]

Entrepreneurs associated with the Munster Plantation tried publications to attract investors and settlers. Fertile land and forests, and even the potential for rabbit breeding, were announced in Robert Payne's *Brief Description of Ireland*; another offered interested parties the vision of iron and copper for mining, fish in plenty, and for timber, 'yewe trees hanginge upon the water syde a 1000 in a place'.[31] The new communities in Munster had a large investment in livestock, and made efforts to clear the land and enclose fields for arable production. Contemporaries complained that settlers preferred becoming 'grasiers, maltmen and grey merchants' of agricultural produce, yet the only export definitely associated with the colony, David Quinn claimed, was timber for barrel making, an important and profitable niche.[32] The common exports of wool, tallow, and hides were products of a pastoral economy, and could derive from native Irish lands as readily as English. It seems that many grantees turned from the difficult capital development of an agricultural economy like that of England to a simpler exploitation of natural resources, above all the plentiful timber that was in such high demand in the home country.

With Irish resistance continuing into Elizabeth's last years, the Munster Plantation was beset by labour problems. The natives were understandably unwilling to help clear land for English fields. Offered sustenance and wages, they also refused to help move timber that the colonists had cut down, or help them in other areas of exploitation. The frustrated colonists appealed to the government, which took the Stalinesque view that refusal to work was a kind of treason. Yet the Dublin government was equally injurious to the colonists, when it forced tax payments by distress warrants, i.e., confiscations. Even the great landowners were not immune. The sheriff of County Cork took as many as 500 milch cows from Raleigh's farmers for his alleged debts.[33] With such self-damaging policies, it is small wonder the colony never really prospered.

As part of the colonial programme, London had sought to divide Munster into counties, starting with those based on the major medieval towns of Waterford, Cork, and Limerick (see Figure 1.4). The new regime also led to changes in settlements: cities, towns, villages, and elite residences. Irish cities were self governing, untouched by magnates like the Earl of Desmond, though smaller towns were sometimes controlled or even owned by the aristocracy. Cities were undoubtedly affected by the

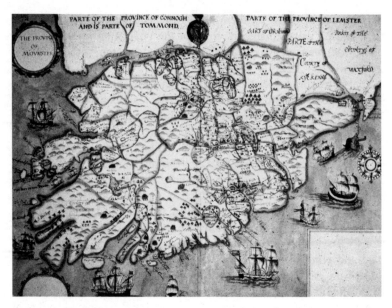

Figure 1.4 Elizabethan Munster. A contemporary copy of Boazio's 1595 map.

political and economic changes of the 1580s and 90s, but this is not yet visible in the archaeological record. The later stages of the Nine Years War that first overthrew the Munster Plantation, and then imposed English rule, did leave traces because until then cities were protected only by medieval walls and gates. Many new fortifications were planned for the cities, and some were constructed before hostilities finally ended. At Cork, a Renaissance citadel called Elizabeth Fort was built *ca.*1600 to both dominate and defend the city (see Figure 1.5).

Smaller towns might show changes wrought by Munster colonization. Existing ones benefitted from new settlement and trade, and some may have outgrown their medieval walls. Both ports and inland towns prospered with little thought of defence, like Buttevant along the road between Limerick and Cork, a target to be plundered and burned in 1598. The Munster colony also saw new towns established. River traffic on the Bride tributary of the Blackwater reached Tallow, which had boasted 120 Englishmen and their families on the eve of its destruction by Tyrone's army. Urban development returned in the early 1600s. Sir Richard Boyle bought Raleigh's estates and others for pennies on the pound. Later becoming the Great Earl of Cork under James, Boyle and other wealthy

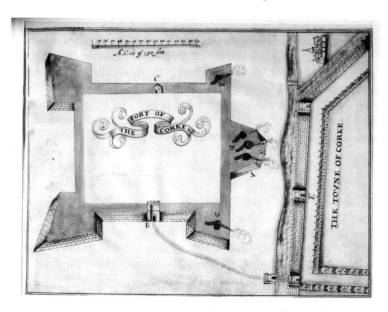

Figure 1.5 Elizabeth Fort at Cork erected in 1603 and rebuilt by Thomas Pynnar in 1626.

landowners would act like modern developers, establishing settlements like Bandon and Baltimore purely for financial profit.

The typical Tudor English village, with cottages clustered around a mill, manor house, and church, did not exist in pre-plantation Munster. The agricultural regime was not one to support nucleated villages. Rather, the ubiquitous *clachan* settlements were small hamlets of fewer than a dozen dwellings. Some of the population was thought to lack permanent settlement. They engaged in transhumance, or 'boolying,' accompanying their herds in a seasonal movement among pasturelands. On Raleigh's lands, however, English settlers established compact villages in various forms, with adjacent fields.

The residences of the colonial elite also dotted the countryside. Government officers and landholding heads of seignories for the most part reoccupied the seats of Irish lordships, adapting or adding to the existing structures. Medieval Ireland had a number of true castles, multi-towered walled enclosures permanently garrisoned for the Crown or a high noble. Most Irish structures termed 'castles', however, are much smaller, comprising a stone residential tower and a wooden or stone hall and service buildings in a 'bawn' walled enclosure. Many of the Munster tower-houses would have been occupied by the English colonial elite. In some cases, the towers were retained, with new Tudor residences erected in the bawn, like the handsome Tudor mansion at Carrick-on-Suir, the seat of the Earl of Ormond, Elizabeth's cousin and part of the ruling establishment (see Figure 1.6).

Elsewhere, tower-houses were incorporated into a new residence, a fortified house, but usually this new building type stood alone in the bawn. Such castle-houses were defended by gun loops, rooftop battlements, and machicolation, and often corner turrets, as at Mallow Castle built by Sir Thomas Norris, President of Munster (see Figure 1.7). Such structures gave sufficient protection against sudden raids, and given the unsettled nature of the Irish countryside, they continued to be built well into the next century. At the same time, expectations of effective control again led leaders to build undefended great houses, the most dramatic example of which is the massive ruin of the governor's palace at Jigginstown, which the absolutist Thomas Wentworth, Lord Strafford, left unfinished for London and the scaffold in 1640 (see Figure 1.8).

Sir Walter Raleigh, Elizabeth's favourite in the 1580s, not only explored the New World and founded settlements there; he also received a huge grant of 42,000 acres in the Blackwater River valley in eastern Munster. Raleigh administered these lands from his seat at Lismore Castle and from his home, since called 'The Myrtles', in the port town of Youghal. Raleigh received most of his Irish income as annual rents from long-term leases. A typical lease to a settler comprised 400 acres of arable land, with all woods, underwoods, waters, weirs, rivers, pools, fords, marshes, moors, bogs, mountains, barren heaths, waste grounds, commons, fowling, fishing, hawking, hunting, and all other profits, commodities, and advantages whatsoever, for £10 per annum and four hens, if required. Reserved for Raleigh were royalties (delegated royal rights) of the property and all wrecks of the sea. The tenant was required to supply one horseman (for military needs), to erect and furnish one mansion or dwelling house, and to enclose with hedge, ditch, and quickset (plantings) 100 acres in good repair and fencing.[34] Further management instructions were given. The settler would receive one penny for each acre converted from waste, and was ordered to leave standing twenty-five trees in every acre that was cut, 'according to custom of England'.[35] Assuming that a mature tree spanned an average of 25 feet, such a programme of timber management would retain about 12.5%, or one-eighth, of each acre.

Raleigh retained direct control of most of his manors, which were divided in small farms as leaseholds, but he did lease some manors to

Figure 1.6 The Elizabethan residence at Ormond Castle, Carrig-on-Suir. One of two medieval tower-houses appears in the background.

Figure 1.7 Mallow Castle, *ca.* 1600, with prominent polygonal corner and entrance towers.

friends and associates. One of these manors, that of Mogeely Castle, went to Raleigh's lieutenant, Henry Pyne. A map, now in the National Library of Ireland, was drawn in 1598 to accompany the re-issue of Pyne's lease, and its accuracy was confirmed by fieldwork there in 1990–93[36] (see Figure 3.4). A village green was probably based upon the forecourt or outer bailey of the castle. English-style houses flanked the 'green' and the road leading south, while others were scattered throughout the neighbourhood. Test excavation and geophysical surveys located the southernmost colonial house opposite the church across the main access route into Mogeely. A 0.7m wide mortar-filled foundation trench would have supported a single-storey structure of timber-framed walling. The building's area, 35 feet (11.6m) by 22 feet (7.3m) internally, and its north–south orientation match the scale and orientation of the colonial house on the map.

Sir Walter Raleigh's tenants at 'Moghelly' were given specific orders to 'dwell in the town ... keep their arms in readiness. ... [and] ... all upon the sound of the drum repair to the castle gate'.[37] Yet the settlement did not develop sufficiently, and the Mogeely map shows that more English had settled in the countryside than at the castle (see Figure 3.6). Their houses appear among native Irish huts or cabins in the surrounding hamlets. To investigate this, the National Committee for Archaeology, for the Office of Public Works, funded the 1992–93 excavations of the Carrigeen

Figure 1.8 The early seventeenth-century palatial residence of Lord Deputy Strafford at Jigginstown.

settlement, northwest of Mogeely Castle. Evidence there suggested a short-lived English occupation of a pre-existing Irish *clachan* hamlet.[38] Although the site had been heavily ploughed in the recent past, patterns of stone scatter indicated the positions of two house platforms, 8m apart, with different cobbled surfaces inside the structures and adjoining yards and paths. Slight traces of clay helped to indicate the line of robbed, 0.75m-wide clay-packed stone walls that formed a two-bay structure with a 5m by 10m interior, and a three-bay structure with interior measurements of perhaps 6.5m by 15m.

Apparently built on a new site, the rectilinear features of the larger structure suggest an English style of construction (see Figure 3.7). The other house platform has features of two clearly distinguishable orientations, the latest of which is parallel to, and presumably contemporary with, the larger building, while the earlier may have been constructed with rounded wall corners typical of the Irish peasant tradition. Although the few stratified finds at Carrigeen offer little information, the architectural indication of cultural change marks the replacement of an Irish 'cabin' with construction more closely identified with the English. It is more likely to indicate the replacement of Irish inhabitants by English colonists than the adoption of English building techniques by pre-existing tenants.

Chapter 3 will more fully discuss colonial settlements, but it should be noted here that the group of houses at Carrigeen appear on the map as both English and Irish. This suggests a slow conversion of *clachan* to hamlet, though not necessarily a slow replacement of population. The Mogeely Castle estate map also presents an example of colonial settlement *de novo*. On part of the neighbouring manor of Curraglass was a newly founded settlement. The Curraglass community was laid out with some regularity as a crossroads (or T-junction) settlement, a form that it still follows (see Figure 3.8). On the map, houses fronted the streets and were clearly aligned to them. Here, some English-style houses, most likely those of more prosperous settlers, were located outside the village, apparently on their own landholdings. Disappointingly, excavations at the one unoccupied site in Curraglass found that an eighteenth-century farmyard and buildings had destroyed evidence of the Tudor house.[39]

The Mogeely estate map also depicted two Irish *clachan* villages that comprised scattered cabins. Both were clustered by streams on the edge of the wooded uplands, clearly excluded from the newly enclosed fields on good soils by the valley bottom (see Figure 1.9). This physical exclusion from the new agricultural regime mirrored the exclusion of the native population from the new political regime. Colonization by

Figure 1.9 Glanatore native Irish community in 1598. Detail from Mogeely Estate map.

displacement meant that the Irish peasantry suffered for the rebellious actions of their lords, but this applied unevenly. On Desmond lands, the Irish could participate only where English settlers were few; on other lordships the traditional landholding and settlement patterns remained in place. Despite the limited immigration, English grantees often did impose their farming system or exploit timber and mineral resources, which suggests that under other circumstances the Munster colonists would have become permanent residents, and the Irish permanently displaced. Yet among the colonists themselves, the desire for independent farmsteads created such strong social and economic pressures that the planned towns and villages of the Elizabethan Plantation could not resist the trend toward dispersed settlement, a fatal choice, given the native population that remained.

Colonization relies upon military superiority, and after 1598 the conquest of Ireland became fixed government policy. Military experience and leadership was important to the elite that constituted both national government and colonial rule, and this should be reflected in its archaeology. It now seems that the Elizabethan wars, not the Cromwellian campaigns, began the replacement of traditional forms of military construction by those of Renaissance Italy. English armies in Ireland, as in the Netherlands, employed regular designs for encampments and fortifications. Unfortunately, modern suburban development and deep

Figure 1.10 Excavation of Renaissance-style polygonal defences at Dunboy Castle, repairs here made in the siege of 1602.

ploughing have substantially eliminated earthworks that could have corroborated the illustrated siegeworks and fortifications of the most important military operation in the Nine Years War, the 1601 siege of Kinsale. The account of the Elizabethan victories, *Pacata Hibernia,* published by Sir Thomas Stafford in 1633, probably used the original maps and texts of Sir George Carew, a leader of that campaign.[40] Other maps survive from the final campaigns of the Elizabethan wars, and those sites have great archaeological potential for comparative work in Ulster.[41]

The last Munster stronghold to fall to Elizabeth's armies was Dunboy Castle, and the 1989 excavations there revealed that the medieval tower-house, or keep, and its bawn enclosure (see Figure 1.10) had been improved in 1601–02 with new defences designed to resist the English army's artillery.[42] The tower-house had been reduced in height and was protected by a bastioned defensive wall with earthen ramparts. These changes, however, proved inadequate to the heavy bombardment it received by land and sea, and the garrison retreated to the tower-house. When called to surrender, the defenders refused, and most died when their stronghold was stormed. The tower-house was then blown up to prevent future use against the Crown.

Jacobean colonization

Following the English victory at Kinsale in 1601, the colonization of Munster resumed, but few of the original landholders continued into the new century. The poet Edmund Spenser died soon after fleeing his burning house in 1598. Sir Walter Raleigh is said to have 'disposed of his grant in disgust', and settlers in Munster after 1601 were 'almost lost among the surviving native population'.[43] Richard Boyle, Secretary of the Munster Council, seized this and other opportunities to amass the largest landholding in Munster.[44] Boyle, whom King James soon knighted and later raised to the peerage as Earl of Cork, provided leadership for the second plantation of Munster. There was little resistance by the Irish or by the Catholic 'Old English' to the new rulers, whose power was based upon the English army's total victory. The government no longer maintained the original scheme for settlement, and the Elizabethan attempt to moderate landholding by limits on size and number of seignories was disregarded for the seventeenth-century rule of competitive cupidity.

Steven Ellis has argued that the sixteenth-century Tudor policy of conquest did more harm than good. The economies of the English areas were weakened by battle damage, army exaction and quartering, and heavy taxation. 'By the end of the century Irish trade interests were increasingly being subordinated to English interests in accordance with contemporary mercantilist theories'.[45] As regulations to protect industries, he cited licenses for export wool and in 1569 additional duties on the export of untanned hides, an industry that he contended was strong until superseded by a greater emphasis on timber exploitation in the early Stuart period. Flocks, unprocessed wool, and woollen and linen yarn continued to be exported to England, while the cloth industry declined in the seventeenth century. Bypassing the town merchants, large landowners drew immediate profit by exporting primary products such as timber. Other investors found a fishing industry in slow decline as the Newfoundland banks were developed.[46] For David Quinn, the problem for the colonists was how to find capital for developing a land without gold, silver, or 'tropical riches'; for Aidan Clarke, a key weakness of colonial economic strategies was 'a constant tendency to visualize industrial undertakings as a form of plantation, imposed upon the local environment rather than emerging from it'.[47] Warning against too readily finding an economic model for Plantation Ireland, however, Raymond Gillespie has argued that because Ireland was not a *tabula rasa* for settlement and its labour force did not depend upon slavery or indentured servitude, colonization and economic development there did not match the pattern of either the Atlantic World or the European economies.[48]

Yet prosperity was certainly evident in the seventeenth century, and not too many years after Raleigh had sold off all his Irish properties. New men like Richard Boyle found fortunes easier to make under James. If large enough sums came to him from Ireland, the king was willing to maintain a military force while dropping Elizabeth's restrictions on large landholdings. Boyle's fortune used Raleigh's exceptional estate of three and one-half seignories as the basis for huge property holdings. He converted short-term leases to long-term, then converted long-term leases to freehold, and eventually to common socage and fee simple, that is, in complete ownership without any feudal obligations to the Crown.[49] Boyle soon became the richest man in Ireland, and England, too. He reinvested his landed income in development projects, establishing new towns as ports, markets, and industrial centres like the iron works at Tallow. The seventeenth- and even eighteenth-century economic success of southern Ireland, and especially County Cork, was in part due to Richard Boyle's tremendous wealth and power. He and other Anglo-

Figure 1.11 Map of Baltimore, depicting harbour, castle, town, and adjacent dwellings in the 1630s.

Irish land magnates wisely applied the resources of timber, fish, beef, and butter to the expansionary English commerce looking across the Atlantic to a nascent British Empire.

Although the Jacobean Plantation of Munster often reoccupied earlier settlements, some of the opportunists growing rich from abandoned holdings chose to establish new towns. Sir Thomas Crooke in 1605 acquired land at Baltimore to establish a community that thrived on southwest Ireland's privateering and smuggling trade.[50] Baltimore was fully English, receiving its borough charter in 1612.[51] Inspection of the topographic features at Baltimore permits the 1632 map of the town (see Figure 1.11) to be interpreted as a planned, rectangular settlement set around an earlier castle, and to the east, a separate, irregular community representing an earlier Irish village.[52] Inland, Sir Richard Boyle founded the town of Bandon. Calling it 'as civil a plantation as most in England', Boyle compared it favorably to the prosperous settlements in Ulster.[53]

Ironically, Sir Arthur Chichester simultaneously compared Ulster favorably to James's new American possessions. His well-known phrase expresses the preference of many for colonization within the British Isles: 'I had rather labour with my hands in the plantation of Ulster than dance or play in that of Virginia.'[54] Archaeological activity in Northern Ireland has taken place under different political circumstances than that within the Republic. On each side of the political border, public majorities have strikingly differing views of their pasts, and these have coloured their governments' interest in archaeology. In the south, proto-colonial archaeology found little support until recently, whilst in the north it was welcomed as a way of verifying the history, and distinctiveness, of the Protestant settlement. This has led to basic urban research at such cities as Derry, Coleraine, and Carrickfergus.[55] The countryside too has been studied, especially the bawn settlements typical of the Ulster plantations of the 1610s, some of which, such as Bellaghy and Tully Castle, have been partially restored and opened to the public. It was hoped that the deserted Plantation village of Salterstown would provide useful information to compare with American colonial settlements, where early colonial sites of a single, brief occupation are not uncommon. The test excavations at Salterstown, however, found a lengthy and complicated occupation history that belied the documents.[56] This evidence, like that found at the Raleigh sites in County Cork, suggests a greater intensity of site use than in the New World. One explanation is that the numbers in Ireland were greater than those in the Americas until the rising tide of the Great Migration during and after the 1640s. Another plausible explanation for this difference is the presence of an ever-expanding colonial frontier in America, a westward moving edge of new settlement that continually diluted the population in established colonial communities. In Ireland, new areas for plantation did open up, but only sporadically, and they were dispersed around the island, e.g., Ulster, Wexford, and Connaught in the seventeenth century.

Notes

1 John Dee, *The Perfecte Arte of Navigation* (London, 1577; repr. Amsterdam, New York, 1968), p. 8.

2 R. Dunlop, 'The Plantation of Munster, 1584-1589', *English Hist. Rev.* 3 (1888), pp. 250–69; D. B. Quinn, 'The Munster Plantation: problems and opportunities', *J. Cork Hist. and Archaeol. Soc.* 71 (1966), pp. 19–40.

3 The felicitous phrase comes from K. S. Bottigheimer, *English Money and Irish Land* (Oxford, 1971), p. 1.

4 For histories, see N. Canny, *The Elizabethan Conquest of Ireland: A Pattern Established 1567-76* (Hassocks, Sussex, 1976; New York, 1977); Steven G. Ellis, *Tudor Ireland: Crown, Community and the Conflict of Cultures. 1470-1603* (London and New York, 1985); and C. Lennon, *Sixteenth-Century Ireland: The Incomplete Conquest* (New York, 1995). For Protestantism, see M. MacCarthy-Morrogh, *The Munster Plantation* (Oxford, 1986), pp. 190–7; and Ute Lotz-Heumann, 'Confessionalism in Ireland: periodisation and character, 1534-1649', pp. 24–53 in Alan Ford and John McCafferty (eds), *The Origins of Sectarianism in Early Modern Ireland*, (Cambridge, 2005). For archaeology, see J. P. Mallory and T. E. McNeill (eds), *The Archaeology of Ulster from Colonization to Plantation* (Belfast, 1982); D. Power, 'The archaeology of the Munster plantation', pp.197–201, and B. Lacy, 'The archaeology of the Ulster plantation', pp. 201–5, in M. Ryan (ed.), *The Illustrated Archaeology of Ireland* (Dublin, 1991). A broad, but comprehensive study of post-medieval archaeology in the Munster area appeared too late to be incorporated in this volume: Colin Breen, *An Archaeology of Southwest Ireland, 1570-1670* (Dublin, 2007). At the same time, Thomas Herron and Michael Potterton have released a collection of papers bringing fresh insights on how Renaissance themes were manifested in Ireland under the Tudors and Stuarts: *Ireland in the Renaissance, c. 1540-1660* (Dublin, 2007).

5 A. L. Rowse explained that his *Expansion of Elizabethan Europe* (London, 1955) was not anti-Puritan, but rather anti-extremist, whilst at the same time noting that its 'marked western bias' properly reflected the importance of those events upon later centuries. (pp. vii, viii). Many works have examined how social, economic, and most importantly political factors directed or retarded the beginnings of English expansion; among them are J. B. Black, *The Reign of Elizabeth 1558-1603* (Oxford, 1994), J. Guy, *Tudor England* (Oxford, 1990), and L. B. Smith, *The Elizabethan World* (New York, 1966, repub. 1972).

6 'The ambition both in Ulster and in Bermuda and Virginia was the creation of model societies', according to Nicholas Canny, but the actual 'trial-and-error efforts of the subjects of the British Crown throughout the course of the seventeenth century can indeed be considered the Origins of Empire', pp. 9, 32 in 'The origins of empire: an introduction', pp. 22–33 in N. Canny (ed.) *The Origins of Empire: British Overseas Enterprise to the Close of the Seventeenth Century*, Vol.1, Oxford History of the British Empire (Oxford and New York, 1998).

7 E. P. Cheney, 'Some English conditions surrounding the settlement of Virginia', *American Hist. Rev.* 12 (1907), pp. 509–28. The citation is from p. 512.

8 See V. Stefansson, *The Three Voyages of Martin Frobisher* (London, 1938).

9 W. A. Kenyon, *Tokens of Possession. The Northern Voyages of Martin Frobisher* (Toronto, 1975) and W. W. Fitzhugh and J. S. Olin, *Archaeology and the Frobisher Voyages* (Washington, 1993).

10 See D. B. Quinn, *The Voyages and Colonizing Enterprises of Sir Humphrey Gilbert* (London, 1940).

11 E. Klingelhofer, 'Geophysics and the search for Raleigh's outposts', in Basil Reed (ed.), *Archaeological Geoinformatics, Case Studies from the Caribbean* (Tuscaloosa, Alabama, 2008).

12 D. B. Quinn, *Set Fair for Roanoke: Voyages and Colonies 1584-1606* (Chapel Hill and London, 1985) is the last distillation of Professor Quinn's views on Raleigh's colony. A more recent encompassing of proto-colonial activities in both Carolina and Virginia is I. Nöel Hume, *The Virginia Adventure. Roanoke to James Towne: An Archaeological and Historical Odyssey* (New York, 1994). The argument that the earthworks might date to the eighteenth century was made to encourage the resumption of excavation there (Nöel Hume, personal comm., 2007), which has had the intended effect.

13 Klingelhofer, 'Geophysics'.

14 See Raymond Gillespie, 'The Transformation of the Irish Economy 1550-1700', pp. 24–6. in Roebuck, Peter and Dickson, David (gen. eds), *Studies in Irish Economic and Social History* (Dundalgan, 1991).

15 Kenneth Nicholls, 'Gaelic society and economy in the High Middle Ages', pp 397–438 in T. W. Moody *et al.* (eds), *Medieval Ireland*. Vol. 2, *A New History of Ireland* (Oxford, 1967), pp. 417, 421. For port towns, see R. A. Butlin, 'The land and the people', pp. 141–86 in T. W. Moody *et al.* (eds), *Modern Ireland 1534-1691*. Vol. 3, *A New History of Ireland* (Oxford, 1976).

16 Gillespie, *Irish Economy*, p. 6.

17 F. Emery, 'The farming regions of England', pp. 1–112, and A. Everitt, 'The marketing of agricultural produce', pp. 466–592, in J. Thirsk (ed.), *The Agrarian History of England and Wales. Vol. IV 1500-1640* (Cambridge, 1967), pp. 73, 78, 129, 136, 527–9.

18 *Ibid.*, pp. 186, 226, 640, 646. For additional observations on the seventeenth-century economy, with details on Munster, see Gillespie, *Irish Economy*, pp. 5, 6. For Ulster, see A. Clark, 'The Irish economy, 1600–1669', pp. 168-86 in Moody *et al.* (eds), *Modern Ireland*, especially pp. 176–83; and R. C. Nash, 'Irish Atlantic trade in the seventeenth and eighteenth centuries', *William and Mary Quarterly*, 3rd ser., 42 (1985), pp. 329–56. For the British context, see R. Davies, *English Overseas Trade 1500-1700*, (London, 1973).

19 Canny, *Elizabethan Conquest*, pp. 33–4.

20 D. B. Quinn, 'Ireland and sixteenth century European expansion', *Irish Hist. Studies* 1 (1958), pp. 20–32.

21 R. Dunlop, 'The Plantation of Leix and Offaly', *English Hist. Rev.* 6 (1891), pp. 61–96.

22 PRO MPF 277, reproduced in P. Kerrigan, *Castles and Fortifications in Ireland 1485-1945* (Cork, 1995), pp. 31–2, Fig. 18.

23 Canny, *Elizabethan Conquest*, pp. 78–82.

24 D. B. Quinn, 'Sir Thomas Smith (1513-1577) and the beginnings of English colonial theory', *Proceedings of the American Philosophical Society* 88 (1944), pp. 543–60.

25 'All Irishmen, especially native in that country, which commonly be called churls, that will plow the ground and bear no kind of weapon nor armor, shall be greatly entertained, and for their plowing and labor shall be well rewarded with great provision': Historical Manuscripts Commission, *De l'Isle and Dudley MSS*. ll, pp.12–15; quoted in D. B. Quinn, *Elizabethans and the Irish* (New York, 1964), p. 108.

26 *Ibid.*

27 The settling of Munster is most fully treated in MacCarthy-Morrogh, *The Munster Plantation*. See also Quinn, 'Munster Plantation'.

28 J. Brewer (ed.) *Calendar for State Papers Relating to, Ireland, vol. 2, 1574–1585*, pp. 588–9.

29 A. J. Sheehan, 'The population of the plantation of Munster: Quinn reconsidered', *J. Cork*

Hist. and Archaeol. Soc. 87 (1982), pp. 107–17.

30 Anthony M. McCormack, 'The social and economic consequences of the Desmond rebellion of 1579-83', *Irish Hist. Studies* 43, No. 133 (May 2004), pp. 1–15.

31 R. Payne, *Brief Description of Ireland* (London, 1589); and 'Henry Cuffe to the Consistory of the Dutch Church in London, 30 Nov 1603', extract in D. B. Quinn 'The Munster Plantation', citations on p. 35.

32 Quinn, 'Munster Plantation', p.32.

33 J. Pope Hennessy, *Sir Walter Ralegh in Ireland* (London, 1883), p. 57, quotes Raleigh's complaint that the plantation had lost colonists because the Governor awarded Irish claimants: 'the doting Deputie has dispeopled me'. Raleigh had considerable trouble with Lord Deputy Sir William Fitzwilliam over his claims to property and timber exports, for which see D. B. Quinn, *Ralegh and the British Empire* (Harmondsworth, 1947, repr. 1973), pp. 114–19.

34 Pope Hennessy, *Ralegh in Ireland*, p. 234–7.

35 *Ibid.*, p. 238.

36 For the Mogeely Map (National Library of Ireland MS 22,028), see J. H. Andrews, *Irish Maps* (Dublin, 1978), plate 12, and *Plantation Acres* (Belfast, 1985) p. 43; for the excavations, see E. Klingelhofer, 'Elizabethan settlements at Mogeely Castle, Curraglass, and Carrigeen, Co. Cork (Part I)', *J. Cork Hist. and Archaeol. Soc.* 104 (1999), pp. 97–110, and 'Elizabethan settlements (Part II)', 105 (2000), pp. 155–74.

37 *Calendar for State Papers Relating to, Ireland, vol. 3, 1598–1600*, pp., p.125.

38 See Klingelhofer, 'Elizabethan settlements (Part II)', pp.157–73.

39 See Klingelhofer, 'Elizabethan settlements (Part II)', pp.155–7.

40 T. Stafford, *Pacata Hibernia* (London, 1633).

41 See G. A. Hayes-McCoy, *Ulster and other Irish Maps c. 1600* (Dublin, 1964); Lacy, 'Ulster Plantation'; and Kerrigan, *Castles and Fortifications*.

42 E. Klingelhofer, 'The Renaissance fortifications at Dunboy Castle, 1602: a report on the 1989 excavations' *J. Cork Hist. and Archaeol. Soc.* 97 (1992), pp. 85–96.

43 Cheney, 'Some English conditions', p. 516.

44 Raleigh seems to have tried to dispose of his estates before the rebellion in Munster; see Quinn, *Ralegh and the British Empire*, p. 123. On 7 December 1602, he did sell his now-ruined holdings to Boyle for £1500, of which he received only £500, King James then demanding the remainder. See Raleigh Trevelyan, *Sir Walter Raleigh* (London, 2002; New York, 2004), pp. 317, 349.

45 S. G. Ellis, Tudor Ireland: Crown, Community and the Conflict of Cultures. 1470-1603 (London and New York, 1985), p. 49.

46 Ellis relies extensively on A. K. Longfield, *Anglo-Irish Trade in the Sixteenth Century* (London, 1929), pp. 71–93.

47 Quinn, *Elizabethans and Irish*, p. 117; Clarke, 'Irish economy', p. 182.

48 Gillespie, *Irish Economy*, pp. 59–60.

49 T. O. Ranger, 'Richard Boyle and the making of an Irish fortune, 1588-1614', *Irish Hist. Studies* 10 No. 39 (1957), pp. 257–97.

50 MacCarthy-Morrogh, *Munster Plantation*, pp. 215–17.

51 R. Caulfield, *The Council Book of Kinsale* (Guildford, Surrey, 1879), p. xxxii; H. Barnby, 'The Sack of Baltimore', *J. Cork Hist. and Archaeol. Soc.* 74 (1969), pp. 106–7.

52 E. J. Priestly, 'An early 17th century map of Baltimore', *J. Cork Hist. and Archaeol. Soc.* 89 (1984), pp. 55–7.

53 Quoted in D. Townshend, *The Life and Letters of the Great Earl of Cork* (London, 1904), p. 44.

54 Quoted in G. Morton, *Elizabethan Ireland* (London, 1971), p 101.

55 See B. Lacy, 'Archaeology of Ulster', in Ryan (ed.), *The Illustrated Archaeology.*

56 O. Miller, 'Interim report on excavations at Salterstown, Northern Ireland', *Proto-Colonial Research* (1989), pp. 8–12.

2

Elizabethan fortifications in Ireland

> Went you to conquer? And have so much lost
> Your self, that what in you was best and most,
> Respective friendship, should so quickly dye?
> In publique gaine my share'is not such that I
> Would loose your love for Ireland ...
> Lett not your soule ...
> It self unto the Irish negligence submit.
>
> John Donne, 1599[1]

Ireland began Elizabeth's reign as a kingdom under the English Crown, and ended it as a quasi-colony. In a process that continued well into the seventeenth century, land available for colonization was provided by confiscations at each act of rebellion, and region by region the island was pacified by new fortifications. Irish religious disaffection followed a growing Calvinist influence in the established Church of England, but the actual breakdown of loyalty was caused by new English arrivals acquiring administrative posts, opportunists who disregarded traditional allegiances and Celtic laws. Fortifications provided a military solution to a political problem. Military technology evolved prodigiously in the sixteenth century, and the new regime in Dublin benefitted from advances in Renaissance warfare.[2]

Yet the campaign to control and colonize sixteenth-century Ireland was only a part of contemporary English military practices, the most pressing goal of which was to defend against other nation states.[3] The second half of the century saw English armies defending first Calais in Picardy only months before Elizabeth came to the throne, and soon there-after Le Havre (Newhaven) in Normandy, followed later by campaigns in Scotland, Brittany, and the Netherlands. There was also the defence of the three 'cautionary towns' the Dutch turned over in 1585 as security for Elizabeth's loans to the United Provinces. In her own country, Elizabeth fortified Berwick against the Scots, sought to control the main sea passages with forts in the Channel Isles off Normandy and the Scilly Isles off Cornwall, and erected defences in the southeast against Spanish forces should the Armada prove successful.

Tudor policies

The Tudor dynasty had a difficult time with the Irish, who had been much attached to the Yorkist family of Edward IV and Richard III. Tudor policy was to spend as little money as possible on Ireland, which was unable to supply in taxes and tribute the sums needed for effective government. English strategy therefore was to defend the Pale, a fortified zone 50 miles around Dublin, and to control the rest of the island by using the great lords and walled towns as largely autonomous authorities. But a medieval monarchy presiding over a feudal aristocracy was doomed when the British Isles joined the great movements of the early modern period: violent religious struggles, the growing power of nation states, and competition for overseas trade and lands. Sixteenth-century Ireland was largely ungovernable by modern standards. In 1541 Henry VIII had tried to improve governance by creating a separate monarchy, with a council and parliament in Dublin, but this only antagonized those Irish lords and merchants who were not part of the Dublin establishment. Faced with a French naval threat, Henry fortified the south coast of England with new artillery forts, but Ireland was not given effective new coastal fortifications until a Spanish invasion materialized in 1601.[4]

The first modern, military-backed colonization of Ireland was proposed in the last years of Henry VIII and was acted upon during the reign of the boy king Edward VI (1547–53). As Lord Protector and regent for his nephew, the Duke of Somerset established two forts on the watershed between the Pale and the Shannon valley, to protect Dublin from raids from the west and connect the Shannon with the walled cities of the southeast, Kilkenny and Waterford. Fort Protector and Fort Governor were garrisoned by English troops, and neighbouring lands were assigned for their support. The reign of Mary and her consort King Philip of Spain saw towns established there, Maryborough and Philipstown, which became the administrative centres for Queen's and King's counties, two new shires cut out of Irish feudal territories. The two towns soon acquired borough status, with licensed markets and self government. Given the turbulent times to come, they never really prospered, even though the forts always maintained some troops as garrisons.

The two forts were sited where small medieval tower-house castles had occupied strategic spots. In both instances, the English followed a static rectangular plan that lacks Renaissance ideas about gun positions for flanking fire and the superiority of polygonal defences. No contemporary drawing survives for the abandoned earthworks of Fort Governor at Philipstown, but one can readily make out clear evidence of a large ditch or moat on two sides. A reused medieval tower-house was centrally located in the 100-metre square enclosure formed by the silted-in ditch and a partially standing circuit wall with a projecting entrance gateway (see Figure 1.3). Philipstown seems to have been built against one side of Fort Governor. The site of the first post-medieval English colonial settlement, Fort Governor is fortunately under no immediate threat of destruction.

Fort Protector in a contemporary drawing shows both the reuse of an old tower-house castle, and the new construction of a round bastion. The original 'forte of Mariborough' had a rectangular 'castell' at one corner of a walled enclosure with labelled measurements of 100 yards by 120 yards (91m by 109.2m); the round tower is labelled 'Blockhouse' at the opposite corner[5] (see Figure 1.2). Inside the fort stood a single structure that probably served as both administrative centre and garrison quarters. Confusingly drawn in both plan and elevation, the two-storey building had several chimneys and casement windows. Outside the fort, built against a stream, was 'The Brewhouse', another essential facility for English soldiers and settlers. A late Elizabethan map shows that Maryborough had developed on three sides of Fort Protector, and was itself protected by a wall without bastions (see Figure 3.3), but these features have been largely obliterated by the growth of the modern town of Portlaoise.[6]

Elizabeth's reign

Despite the relative success of Queen Mary's efforts in Ireland, her reign is better known for its unprepared involvement in Philip's dynastic struggles with France, especially her government's loss of Calais, the all-important foothold on the Continent. Won by the heroic King Henry V, a century and a half of stalwart defence against the French came to an ignominious end when the garrison's supplies ran out. It is said that Philip refused to help Mary retake Calais, and that she died of shame. In any case, Elizabeth, cautious and frugal, found herself queen of an underfinanced and poorly defended realm.

In Ireland the majority of Elizabethan fortifications fall into two groups: those associated with the campaigns along the southern coast

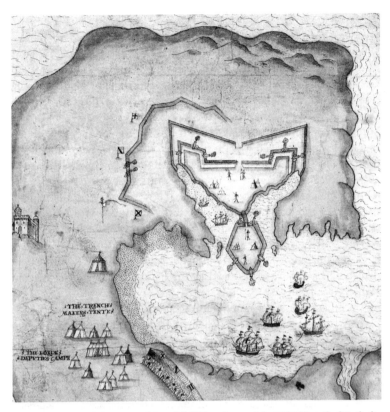

Figure 2.1 Map of the siege of Castel dell'Oro, Smerwick, 1580. Detail of Catholic fortifications and English siegeworks. Notations are 'The Trenche Makers Tente' and 'The Lorde Deputies Campe'.

in Munster, and those associated with the wars in the far north in Ulster. The seriousness of these campaigns changed the practice of warfare in Ireland, even though physical evidence for those changes is limited. The Irish themselves left little in the way of fieldworks, relying on medieval castles or the dense forests to protect them. After years of ambushes and surprise attacks, the English army did begin to entrench themselves on campaign. During siege operations, large earthwork systems became standard practice.

Two short-lived expeditions of Spanish and allied troops generated a number of campaign fieldworks in southern Ireland. The first was in 1580, at Smerwick Bay on the Dingle peninsula. There, answering the

Papal call to free Ireland from England's heretical queen, 600 Italians and Spaniards erected defences on a small promontory. They were soon overwhelmed by English land and naval cannonades. Tragically, because this force finally surrendered unconditionally, the English commander, Lord Grey, with his secretary Edmund Spenser and captain Walter Raleigh, took advantage of the rules of war, massacring all the soldiers and keeping the officers for ransom. The earthworks remain, though damaged by bombardment and slighting, and by cliff erosion. The commander, Bastian di San Joseppi, fortified a place he called 'il Castel dell'Oro', mounting cannon on a cliff-edge promontory, protected by a deep fosse, probably prehistoric.[7] Beyond the promontory, his land defences comprised a linear Italianate design of two half-bastions, with orillons or rounded flanks, each mounting a cannon. The fort was entered by a central gate and bridge across the angled ditch, which seems to have had a covered way or counterscarp. For the English side, a large unfortified camp, a long, irregular trench, and several batteries firing on the Papal fort are depicted in a picture map drawn by the naval commander Sir William Winter[8] (see Figure 2.1).

The other recorded example of Elizabethan fieldworks in Munster took place twenty years later. In 1598, the Irish in the south joined the revolt in Ulster led by Hugh O'Neill, Earl of Tyrone. The sudden attack devastated the English colonists outside the walled cities. Nearly every town, manor, and castle was overrun in Munster. In response, Elizabeth first sent over her court favorite, the Earl of Essex, who was unable to suppress the rebellion. After his disgrace, the command fell to the able and energetic Charles Blount, Lord Mountjoy. In two years he crushed the revolt in the south and neutralized O'Neill in the north. The decisive battle of the campaign in Munster took place around Christmas 1601, at Kinsale on the south coast.[9] A Spanish expeditionary force had occupied the walled town, waiting for Tyrone's forces to arrive from Ulster, but it was besieged for weeks by land and its sea access closed by a naval blockade. When O'Neill's army did arrive, Mountjoy's heavy cavalry intercepted the lightly armed Irish footsoldiers outside Kinsale. O'Neill's army was destroyed in a few hours, and the isolated Spanish garrison surrendered soon thereafter. Kinsale reminds us of the danger of relying too much upon Renaissance prints. A near-contemporary German woodcut appears to have accurate details of the siege, but it is totally fanciful.[10] There are more accurate illustrations, however. The military engineer Paul Ive left a drawing of an early stage of the siege, and Baptista Boazio drew a more complete record, which was reproduced in Thomas Stafford's *Pacata Hibernia* some years

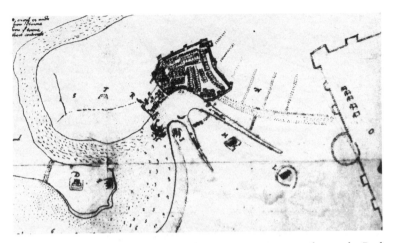

Figure 2.2 Map of Siege of Kinsale, 1601. Contemporary copy of a map by Paul Ive.

later.[11] The recent study of the Battle of Kinsale by Hiram Morgan and his associates has supplied more information and analysis of maps of the siege.[12]

The right side of Ive's map shows part of the English army's camp, drawn at a larger scale than Kinsale and the natural features (see Figure 2.2). The details of Ive's camp are similar to those of the two camps drawn by Boazio, both of which follow textbook examples ultimately drawn from Italian practice[13] (see Figure 2.3). Each is rectangular, having bastions at the corners and often a small rectangular projection midway on a side. The bastions are usually angular, but one corner gate was flanked by round bastions. Boazio depicts two kinds of batteries, one a typical linear construction either straight or bow-shaped, and another more fully enclosed, offering greater protection for the gunners in exposed positions. The first type appear at D, F, H, R, and S. The map depicts three artillery batteries of the enclosed type. The 'first battery' at B is nearly circular with a slight wing; it looks like Mountjoy used pre-existing walls, perhaps of an early medieval ringfort or religious enclosure. The 'second battery' at C is rectangular, with three bastions, one more rectilinear than angular, one a half-bastion, and one round. The 'new battery' at O consists of a linear front and a three-sided enclosure on the rear, with two round flankers.

The Kinsale earthworks include two sconces located some distance from the main encampments to control the river. The smaller is rectangular with four angular or rectilinear corner bastions. The larger one,

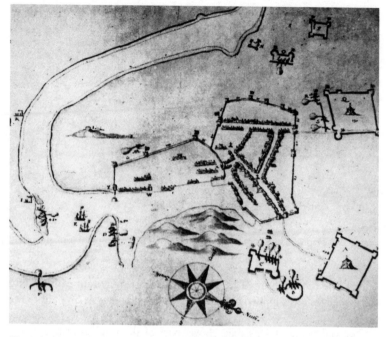

Figure 2.3 Map of Siege of Kinsale, 1601, by Baptista Boazio, published in *Hibernia Pacata*, 1633.

identified as serving a cavalry troop, is square, with angular bastions at three corners and a half-bastion on the fourth. Nothing of these entrenchments appears on the ground today. Several centuries of urban growth have spread out from this popular resort town. One earthwork that does remain, though, is at L, the Spanish-held 'mount' upon Compass Hill, the highest point of ground here. A low mound survives in pasture; its origins could be a prehistoric tumulus.[14] The variety of forms of English defences at Kinsale may not necessarily be attributed to map makers' fancy. The professional Boazio is unlikely to have benefitted by filling his drawing with inaccuracies. There were an unusual number of senior field commanders at the siege, and perhaps their individual construction of siegeworks is the reason for a lack of standardization.

A secondary phase of the Kinsale campaign was the reduction of several castles occupied by Spanish troops along the southwest coast. The surrender terms at Kinsale required that these positions be delivered to the English; this happened everywhere except Dunboy Castle. The Irish

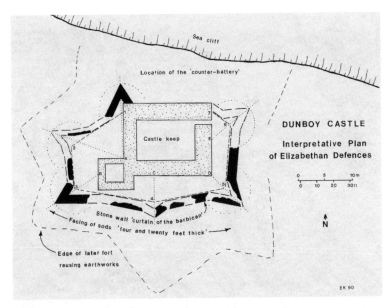

Figure 2.4 Interpretive plan of Dunboy Castle 1602 defences.

managed to seize control of this refortified site before the Spanish could surrender it. This last stronghold in the south was besieged, bombarded, and stormed in June 1602. As depicted in *Pacata Hibernia*, the topographic details are generally correct, but the castle itself is incorrectly drawn. Archaeological excavations have revealed that all elements of the defences were rectilinear, not curved, and that the final state of Dunboy was no doubt Spanish-designed as a nearly symmetrical, bastioned fort around a tower-house that had been reduced in height to present less of a target[15] (see Figure 2.4).

This Renaissance fort was a response to the English army's adoption of siege artillery, with field guns and borrowed ship's cannon. Thick earthen ramparts protected its interior stone revetment wall from bombardment. Angled bastions helped deflect shot as well, but their symmetrical placement was more important in providing 360 degrees firing capability. Designed either by Spanish expeditionary forces or by Irish officers experienced in the French religious wars (or by a combination of the two), it reveals that even the enemies of the Tudor plantations employed Renaissance engineering. Fatally, the designer did not see fit to reduce the height of the tower-house adequately; English batteries soon brought down so

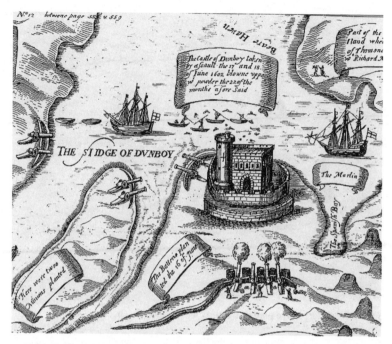

Figure 2.5 Picture map of Siege of Dunboy, 1602, published in *Hibernia Pacata*, 1633. Further distant are a sconce and camp.

much debris into the interior of the fort that the main defences had to be abandoned. Nevertheless, English troops incurred heavy losses when storming the undamaged bottom level of the tower-house.

The Dunboy print shows English fieldworks comprising three linear gun battery entrenchments, as well as a camp, and a small sconce (Figure 2.5). The camp is rectangular, with an unusual central division. It has round corner bastions and one round bastion in the middle of a long side, a kind of short-hand version of the Kinsale Renaissance-style camps. The sconce is square, without flankers. Landscaping and forestry activities unfortunately have removed all traces of these earthworks, so their details cannot be checked. This drawing is more primitive than Boazio's of Kinsale, and one ought to treat with caution the specifics of these fortifications, given the known errors in its depiction of Dunboy Castle.

Ulster campaign forts

The Nine Years War was resolved when in the first years of the 1600s Lord Mountjoy established a series of fortifications that 1) controlled the Ulster countryside and prevented supplies from reaching the rebel forces, and 2) neutralized O'Neill's ability to strike suddenly at isolated units of the English army. Just as the Jacobean colonization of Ulster left a series of illustrations by Thomas Raven, so these earlier military operations were also well recorded. Maps and drawings, often by the cartographer Richard Bartlett, include details of English fortifications, and from a selection of these we may observe the frequency by which certain plans or components were used. Similar to the siege of Dunboy is a view, by an unknown and unprofessional hand, of the 1594 siege of Enniskillen Castle[16] (see Figure 2.6). It shows the linear trenches of two English batteries, as well as two camps of square plan, but without indications of the earthworks that should have enclosed them. The two entrances lay at opposite corners, similar to the corner entrance noted above at a Kinsale camp.

A more problematic English fieldwork in Ulster is the Blackwater Fort. The Blackwater River served as a natural barrier between areas that the

Figure 2.6 Picture map of the Siege of Enniskillen Castle, 1594. Copyright British Library Board, BL Cotton MS. Augustus I. ii. 39.

English army could patrol and the heart of Tyrone's lands. An important strategic objective during the Nine Years War, the main ford across the Blackwater exchanged hands several times. The English army constructed earthworks at the ford, which were then seized by O'Neill, who is said to have destroyed them but later erected there one of the few Irish fieldworks. Alarmed, the Governor, Lord Burgh, successfully attacked the rebels in 1597 but died soon after constructing a new fort nearby. This advance position proved to be too isolated and trying to resupply it in 1598 Sir Henry Bagenal was ambushed at the Yellow Ford and his army destroyed. A well-known drawing purports to be an eye-witness account of Burgh's victory in the previous year[17] (see Figure 2.7). While it follows the general account of the battle, it varies at several points from the official descriptions, which suggest that the drawing may have been made on the site, but some time after the battle. The English reported that there was a simple, 'plashed' or woven palisade along the river bank. The drawing does in fact represent a sort of palisade in the front of the fort, which was earth-built, with two round flankers. The English reported this, and the fact that the flankers did not actually cover the west end of the ford. It seems that this fort was never intended to block an attack from the east, from across the

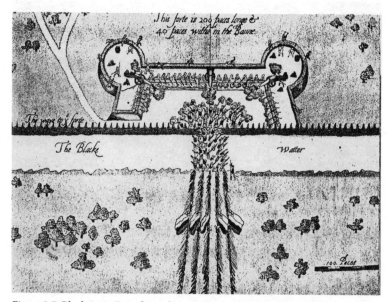

Figure 2.7 Blackwater Fort, from the painting at Trinity College Dublin, redrawn by G. A. Hayes-McCoy.

river, but from the west, from O'Neill's side of the Blackwater. The logical explanation is that O'Neill simply reused previous earthworks, adding only the palisade at the river bank. Contrary to the English claims, the Irish probably had no real investment in this fort. Its guard of twenty to forty men soon retreated, giving warning to the main Irish camp nearby, which repulsed Burgh's attempts to advance further.

Blackwater Fort must have been originally designed to face west, and lie open to the ford. It comprised three walls and two round flankers, and

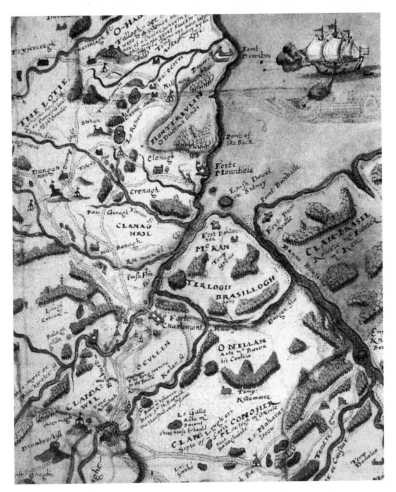

Figure 2.8 Map of Mountjoy's Ulster campaign, by R. Bartlett, 1602–3.

though no ditch is shown on the drawing, the earth for the entire structure would normally have been removed from the ground immediately
outside the walls, resulting in a considerable ditch. A letter describing the
assault does in fact note that the attack overcame several obstacles: the
palisade and the height of the ditches and the earth bank.[18]

When Lord Mountjoy became Lord Deputy, his first construction in
Ulster was Fort Moyry, built in 1601 to control the important pass leading
north from Dundalk. Of conservative design, it comprised a small stone
tower with an earthwork bawn.[19] In 1602 Richard Bartlett drew up a
map, bearing Mountjoy's coat of arms, to illustrate the final campaigns
in Ulster; it is an important source of information on late Elizabethan
defensive construction.[20] It depicts a small-scale view of the area around
the O'Neill seat of Dungannon, including Loch Neagh and the Blackwater valley (see Figure 2.8). It portrays a landscape scarred by war, with
ruined, roofless churches. Red flags apparently indicate English positions.
Flagged tents representing outpost garrisons are sited at important road
junctions. Castles dot the countryside, some flagged as occupied by the
English, others remaining in owners' hands or abandoned. Several types
of English fortifications are also shown. The most common form is that
of a small square enclosure with opposing bastions that usually appear
round, though the small scale makes it hard to be certain in every case.
Four such examples are depicted and named: Fort Ennish Alaghon, Fort
Bunvalle, Fort Bandornan (Bundorian), and Fort O'Donallie. Although
clearly labelled as forts by the English authorities who drew up the map,
the comparatively small size of the earthworks (less than 33m across)
suggests that they would best fall under the category of sconces. This
group of four is the clearest indication of one standard form of military
engineering in Elizabethan Ireland.[21]

Composite forms were also common fortifications in Mountjoy's
campaign. Three forts, all at important strategic centres and built within
months of each other, continued to have garrisons into the seventeenth
century. These 'large hybrids' show added or overlapping defences, apparently from different periods of construction. As the campaign map bears
no other irrelevant details, it may be assumed that all elements of these
defences were functional when the map was drawn up. It may be that
other earthworks at these sites had been disused, perhaps even slighted,
and were not drawn because they were irrelevant to the current state of
the defence works.

Fort Mountnorris, started in 1601, may have reused an ancient ringfort as a circular walled enclosure, its gate covered by a simplified crown

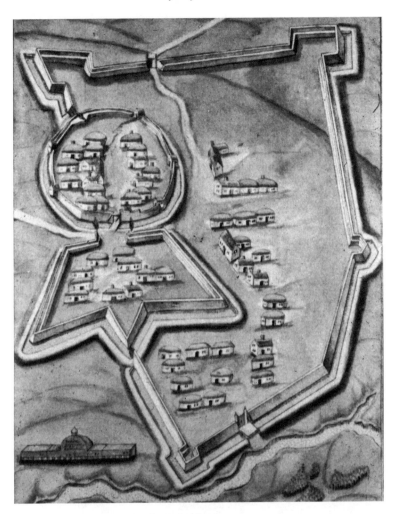

Figure 2.9 Fort Mountnorris, by R. Bartlett.

work, and both flanked by outer defenses that contained four different-shaped bastions (see Figure 2.9). Fort Charlemont, built in 1602, was a square or perhaps trapezoid earthwork 40m across with demi-bastions at each corner (see Figure 2.10). This is a common enough textbook plan, but on one side was a hornwork with a central bastion.[22] Fort Mountjoy appears to have been a five-pointed star-fort, plus closer to Lough Neagh was what looks like a triangular-shaped work.[23] This is unlikely to be a

Figure 2.10 Fort Charlemont by R Bartlett.

Figure 2.11 Projecting corner tower of Fort Mountjoy. Note the brick upper walling and masonry quoins.

battery, as English gunboats controlled the water, and it may have been a surviving portion of a pre-existing earthwork. By 1605 Governor Mountjoy seems to have replaced this entire fort with one of the first brick structures in Ulster. The nearby standing ruins of this newer Fort Mountjoy, once surrounded by its own polygonal earthwork, are perhaps best interpreted as the Lord Deputy's permanent field headquarters, similar to a fortified manor house (see Figure 2.11).

The campaign map shows some other fortifications. At Drumboe, in the north, a flag indicates an English military post, but the plan there looks like a typical Celtic circular enclosure, serving a ruined monastic church. Mountjoy's men must have simply taken over the site as a defended outpost, and did not name it as a fort. The medieval tower-house castle and bawn enclosure of Benburg also appears on the map, but without a flag, indicating that it was not an English outpost. In the subsequent colonization of Ulster, an English owner would replace the tower-house with a manor house, while the bawn received large square corner towers or flankers (see Figure 2.12).

Richard Barlett drew other maps of the Ulster campaign. A large-scale picture-map shows a fortification at Monaghan, erected in 1602.[24] The square-shaped earthwork, 30m across, has triangular bastions or redans centred on each side, resulting in a regular, but unequal, eight-pointed star. Along the ditch line are a counterscarp and outer embankment or glacis, of textbook engineering. This fort probably replaced the small square earthen or rubble-built fort that appears in an inset on the map. The walls of the latter are pierced with many embrasures, serving muskets not artillery, and if not some sort of Irish fort, then it is most likely to have been a temporary redoubt-type structure to protect the troops engaged in constructing Fort Monaghan. It is similar in size and shape to the small square 'artwork' across the river from Fort Charlemont (see Figure 2.10).

Another English fort established to control the countryside appears at the opposite end of the island, in Co. Carlow, by its border with Wexford. Sited at Coolyhune, near St Mullins, on the top of a hill dominating the River Barrow, most of the fort's walls have survived as high as 3.5m,

Figure 2.12 Corner tower of Benburg Castle bawn enclosure.

Figure 2.13 Bastioned starfort at Coolyhune, Co. Carlow. It has a commanding position, but its drystone walls lack an earthen rampart.

although portions of the interior are now covered in concrete to store hay.[25] Coolyhune appears to have been a pentagonal starfort of unusual drystone walling, as no earth component now exists (see Figure 2.13). But even more unusual, it has been identified as the fort erected and garrisoned in 1581 by Captain Anthony Colclough on orders from Sir Henry Wallop, and finally abandoned in 1634. As such, the site would be the earliest known starfort in Ireland, and would prove that Renaissance models of fortifications were used by the English even before their intervention in the Dutch wars. The unusual drystone walling, if not serving to revet lost earthen ramparts (for which there is no ditch), might support the identification of an early, experimental design. However, it should be noted that many starforts were constructed during the seventeenth-century Irish wars, and it needs to be firmly established whether or not it was built by Cromwell's army, even if an earlier structure had stood there.[26]

Other English fortifications

Other fortifications in Ireland were constructed in the late Elizabethan period, or planned then and built in the subsequent reign. They are divided into two classes according to their purpose: modernizing

Figure 2.14 Picture-map of Carrickfurgus, Co. Antrim, *ca.* 1560. Copyright British Library Board: BL Cotton MS I. ii. 42.

medieval urban defences against the Irish, and protecting harbours from the Spanish.

Two centuries of unrest had left the cities of Ireland with good walls and towers as defence against raids by sword-and-shield-bearing foot-soldiers. The age of musket and artillery called for changes, which at first entailed mounting cannon on existing walls and cutting embrasures to

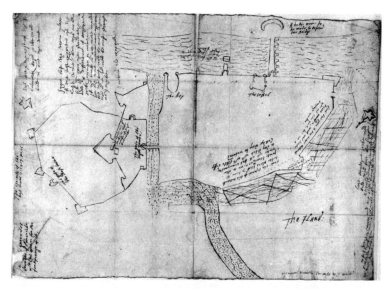

Figure 2.15 Plan of proposed defences for Limerick, by Sir Richard Grenville, *ca.* 1590.

serve them. Such unsophisticated changes are seen in the picture-map of Carrickfurgus, from the third quarter of the century (see Figure 2.14). Where efforts were made to update urban defences at the close of the Elizabethan Wars, the English chose the Italian model of an external citadel to defend and overawe the town. Elizabeth Fort was a masonry polygonal fort overlooking Cork at the end of the queen's reign (see Figure 1.5). Richard Grenville has left us his hand-drafted proposed defensive system for Limerick (see Figure 2.15). His plan employed Renaissance military practices that included oblique lines of defence, starforts, and, across the Shannon bridge from King John's Castle, a 'half-moon' demi-lune earthwork.[27]

London worried about the Spanish threat to the long south and west coastlines, indented with numerous bays and coves, but was especially concerned for the existing ports. For Cork harbour and Kinsale harbour, the military engineer Paul Ive constructed *ca.*1602 polygonal bastioned earthen forts on elevated positions. According to Paul Kerrigan's research, Josiah Bodley, supervising the defences of Ireland for James I, was responsible for altering both defences around 1608–11.[28] For the interior of Ive's vast earthen starfort at Castle Park (later Jamesfort) by Kinsale, he erected a masonry citadel about the size and shape of Fort Charlemont, square

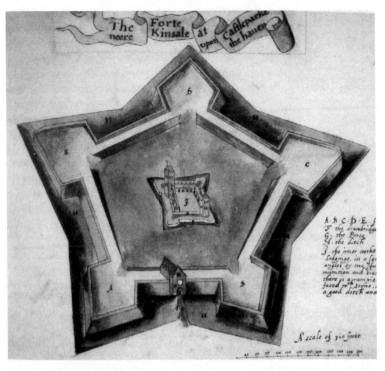

Figure 2.16 Map of Castle Park Fort, Kinsale, Co. Cork, with new interior garrison defences by Sir Josias Bodley, *ca.* 1610. Copyright British Library Board: BL Cotton MS Augustus I. ii. 35.

with demibastions (see Figure 2.16). A shoreline battery or blockhouse there Bodley also added to Haulbowline Fort in Cork harbour, and we may consider this design of a shoreline battery garrisoned and protected by an elevated polygonal fort to be one of the differences between Tudor and Stuart coastal defences. Such an arrangement cannot be attributed to Bodley or even Ive, because a *ca.* 1571 map by Robert Lythe of 'The Fort of Corkbeg not Fynisshed' depicts a bastioned and half-bastioned fort containing a 'A very Fayre House of Stone w'out Rooffe' and 500 feet away, 'A bulwark for the haven mowthe'.[29]

Irish and colonial types of fortification

From Mary's reign to James's, fortifications in Ireland became more complex and more specialized. Some of this may be due to Renaissance influences from Italy and France; some may be drawn from English military experience in the Dutch wars, where fortifications and sieges were the rule, not pitched battles. In the late Elizabethan period, in the Nine Years War, many early forms were still in use, even as new forms became common. More evolution took place under the Stuarts: rounded bastions ceased to be built, and the rectilinear enclosure also became obsolete (except for the ubiquitous residential bawn, which took no other shape). Fortification of both towns and harbours comprised multiple units, employing a defence in depth.

A variety of forts were constructed in Elizabethan Ireland, but some types were rare or appeared shortly after Elizabeth's reign. With a possible exception at Fort Mountjoy, triangular works were not used on their own, but were sometimes an element in a composite defence. Another form was a trapezoid with a pair of angular bastions flanking the short side and a pair of half bastions at the long side. Midway along the 'base' of the trapezoid there was sometimes a small obtuse bastion or battery.[30] A further type, the small quadrangular fort with four half bastions at the corners,

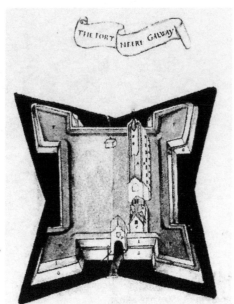

Figure 2.17 St Augustine Fort, Galway, with secondary outer wall by Sir Josias Bodley, *ca.* 1610.

had walls slightly off the rectangular, to provide a field of fire from the half-bastions. Bodley's rebuild at Jamesfort, Castle Park, Kinsale, *ca.* 1610, is the first recorded in Ireland.

Other types were common enough in Ireland to be possible models for later English and colonial defences. The regular pentagonal starfort is claimed to have first appeared in Ireland as early as 1580, but is more likely to have arrived after the start of the seventeenth century. Perhaps because it has the most efficient design, with its walls being also the bastions, this purely Renaissance form has proved to be the most successful, dominating seventeenth- and eighteenth-century fortification.

The quadrangle with corner bastions of angular shape was certainly a favoured shape for small forts and sconces in the Dutch wars and during the English Civil War. It appeared in 1602 as a new fort outside Galway[31] (see Figure 2.17). In the Ulster campaigns that ended the Nine Years War, as we have seen, a small field fort was commonly square with round bastions at opposite corners. In Ireland, opposite flankers go back to the mid-century Tudor forts at Maryborough and Philipstown. Opposing round flankers are little known in the broader European context, but still appear in several seventeenth-century Ulster bawns. Some of the latest round flankers built by English armies were at the Ulster Blackwater

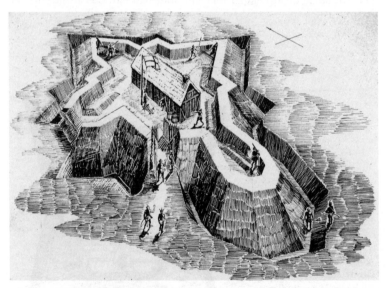

Figure 2.18 Conjectural reconstruction of 'Fort Raleigh', North Carolina, based upon the 1950 excavations.

Figure 2.19 Picture-map of fort built by Ralf Lane at Cape Roja, Puerto Rico, 1585

Fort of 1597, and in the composite bastions of the 1607 James Fort of Virginia.[32]

Another type of small square field fort had at the middle of the walls angular bastions that were smaller and more angled than its right-angled corners. Superficially like a hexagon, the fort at Monaghan and the Elizabethan earthwork on Roanoke Island were of this plan, as with some variations was the temporary fortification Ralph Lane built during the 1585 voyage to Roanoke, to guard salt supplies on a beach in Puerto Rico (see Figures 2.18 and 2.19). A strong Irish connection is that Captain Lane had been given permission by the queen to leave his command in Ireland to serve as governor of Raleigh's colony, and he returned to win a knighthood in the Ulster campaign.

Conclusions

The Netherlands may have been 'a school of war' for the English military, but Ireland was where that schooling was most employed, and it gave its own lessons, too.[33] In Ireland, especially during the Nine Years War, a full variety of fortifications were used. Elizabeth's armies engaged in conflicts ranging from guerrilla warfare to incursions by well-trained Spanish infantry. Campaigns were complex, involving mobile forces and even naval squadrons like Drake's and Levison's. Commanders had to consider the defence of cities and harbours, and the constant problem of supplying garrisons and field armies. Given the increasing skill and dedication of Tyrone's army and its allies, Mountjoy – unlike Essex – was able to maintain and extend Elizabeth's control of Ireland with an agile and aggressive army securely based on new, 'Renaissance' fortifications.

Notes

1 H. W. in Hiber. belligeranti., No. 128 (p. 200) in J. Shawcross (ed.), *The Complete Poetry of John Donne* (Garden City, New York, 1967); 'To Henry Wooton fighting in Ireland' refers to his serving under the Earl of Essex in 1599.

2 See C. Falls, *Elizabeth's Irish Wars* (repr. London, 1970); J. R. Hale, *Renaissance War Studies* (London, 1983), and *War and Society in Renaissance Europe 1520–1620* (London, 1985); and R. Loeber and G. Parker, 'The military revolution in seventeenth-century Ireland', pp. 68–88 in Jane Ohlmeyer (ed.), *Ireland from Independence to Occupation, 1641–1660* (Cambridge, 1995).

3 See H. J. Webb, *Elizabethan Military Science. The Books and the Practice* (Madison, Wisconsin, 1965); C. G. Cruickshank, *Elizabeth's Army*, (Oxford, 2nd edn, 1966); A. L. Rouse, *The Expansion of Elizabethan England* (London, 1955), pp. 327–73 ; and J. R. Hale, 'The defense of the realm, 1485–1558', pp. 367–401, and J. Summerson, 'The defense of the realm under Elizabeth I', pp. 402–14, in H. M. Colvin (ed.), *History of the King's Works Vol. IV 1485–1660 (Part II)*, (London, 1982).

4 S. G. Ellis, *Tudor Ireland: Crown, Community and the Conflict of Cultures* (London and New York, 1985). Ellis considers the attack on great nobles like Kildare a fundamental change in policy throughout Henry's lands in the mid-1530s, p.129.

5 The Maryborough picture-map is preserved in Trinity College Library: TCD MS 1209 (10).

6 PRO MPF 277, reproduced in P. Kerrigan, *Castles and Fortifications in Ireland 1485–1945* (Cork, 1995), pp. 31–2, Fig. 18.

7 Vatican Archives, Nunziatura di Spagna, XXV, f. 370 et seq. A map he sent to Rome is reproduced and discussed in F. M. Jones, 'The plan of the Golden Fort at Smerwick, 1580', *Irish Sword* 2 (1954), pp. 42–3, pl. 5.

8 Reproduced in Michael Swift, *Historical Maps of Ireland* (London, 1999), p. 36.

9 See J. Silke, *Kinsale: The Spanish Intervention in Ireland at the End of the Elizabethan Wars* (New York, 1970); and G. A. Hays–McCoy, *Irish Battles* (London, 1969), pp. 144–73.

10 Reproduced in Silke, *Kinsale*, facing p. 145.

11 A contemporary copy of Paul Ive's map appears in G. A. Hayes-McCoy, *Ulster and other Irish Maps c. 1600* (Dublin, 1964), plate XIII; Baptisto Boazio's map: Hatfield House, II No 38, Cecil MSS 237/41. Both are reproduced in Silke, *Kinsale*, facing pp.128–9.

12 See Hiram Morgan (ed.), *The Battle of Kinsale*, (Bray, Ireland, 2004). He discusses the Ive and Boazio maps retained by the Cecils at Hatfield House, as well as the maps at the National Maritime Museum (probably Boazio) and the National Library of Ireland (Ive), and the Trinity College painting of the battle, which he believed was the basis for the *Pacata Hibernia* print, in Hiram Morgan, 'Contemporary English maps of the siege and battle of Kinsale', *ibid*, pp. 359–63. The Spanish ambassador in London also acquired a map of the siege, less accurate than the others but from the viewpoint of the besieged. See Ciaran O'Scea, 'Spanish map of the siege of Kinsale', *ibid*, pp. 364–5.

13 See, for example: Paul Ive, *The Practise of Fortification* (London 1589), ed. Martin Biddle (Richmond, 1972); and Robert Corneweyle, *The Maner of Fortification of Cities, Townes, Castelles and other Places*, ed. Martin Biddle (Richmond, 1972).

14 Damien Shiels, 'Fort and field: the potential for battlefield archaeology at Kinsale', pp. 33–350 in Morgan (ed.), *Battle of Kinsale*, refers to many of the other fieldworks – English, Spanish, and Gaelic – but is uncertain about Ive's depiction of a Spanish 'mount' on Compass Hill south of the town, and called for future investigation to discover what it could have been. This suggests that intense property development around Kinsale probably consumed the site after my observations in 1989.

15 E. Klingelhofer, 'The Renaissance fortifications at Dunboy Castle, 1602: a report on the 1989 excavations', *J. Cork Hist. and Archaeol. Soc.*, 97 (1992), pp. 85–96, which extends and amends the fieldwork of E. M. Fahy reported in Margaret Gowen, 'Dunboy Castle, Co. Cork', *J. Cork Hist and Archaeol. Soc.*, 83 (1978), pp. 1–49. The archaeological findings largely support and explain the account of the defences presented in Falls, *Elizabeth's Irish Wars*, pp. 319–20.

16 British Library, Cotton MS Augustus I. ii. 39, reproduced in P. D. A. Harvey, *Maps in Tudor England* (Chicago, 1993), p. 63, ill. 43.

17 See Hays-McCoy, *Irish Battles*, pp. 113–15, Ill. 12.

18 *Ibid*.

19 P. Kerrigan, 'Seventeenth century fortifications, forts and garrisons in Ireland: a preliminary list', *The Irish Sword* 14, Nos. 54, 55 (1980–82), pp. 3–24, 135–56; p. 9.

20 PRO, MPF 36. This study, and the number of fortifications discussed, is based on its reproduction in Harvey, *Maps in Tudor England*, pp. 62–3.

21 Paul Kerrigan, *Castles and Fortifications*, p. 53, thinks that these defences are Irish, because of the similarity of their forms to the Irish fortification at Inisloughan (Bartlett, 1602). Yet Inisloughan has two lines of palisades and two wet ditches around the inner earthwork, which is 60m square with flankers 16m across. This is perhaps double the

size of the campaign map forts, which are clearly smaller than the Charlemont fort core, measuring 10m across. The scale of the Irish fortification and its multiple defences argues against its belonging to the group of small sconces.

22 Margaret Gowen, '17th century artillery forts in Ulster', *Clogher Record* 10 (1980) pp. 239–56, notes that Phillips calls it 'a small sconce', p. 250, which should be the small, square wall-and-ditch structure depicted across the river on NLI MS 2656. Kerrigan, *Castles and Fortifications*, pp. 52, 53, 69, notes that Fort Charlemont was built by Mountjoy in 1602 and the town was incorporated in 1613. Bartlett's map shows about forty houses within the defences, but these are not necessarily evidence of civilian presence.

23 This follows Kerrigan's interpretation, *Castles and Fortifications*, p. 54.

24 See Hayes-McCoy, *Ulster and Other Irish Maps*, pp. 16–17, Fig. IX.

25 The fort is discussed by R. Loeber, 'The lost architecture of the Wexford Plantation', in K. Whelan (ed.), *Wexford: History and Society* (Dublin, 1987), p. 174; and by I. Doyle, 'Historical background to Coolyhune Starfort', *Carloviana* (1991), p. 21.

26 I share the views of Paul Kerrigan, *Castles and Fortifications*, pp. 102, 103. Dunboy Castle, for example, was superseded by a Cromwellian starfort.

27 A *ca.* 1590 map of Limerick defences is discussed by Kerrigan, who notes similarities to Grenville's sketch: *ibid*, pp. 43–4.

28 Kerrigan, *Castles and Fortifications*, pp. 60–1. See also his 'Seventeenth century fortifications'; and B. H. St J. O'Neil, *Castle and Cannon: A Study of Early Artillery Fortifications in England* (Oxford, 1960), pp. 78–9, for Ive's work at Cork and Kinsale and the projected plans for the rest of the south coast.

29 PRO MPF 85, reproduced in Swift, *Historical Maps*, p. 27, and in Kerrigan, *Castles and Fortifications*, p. 35, where he attributes the map to Robert Lythe in 1569 and points out the main fort's similarities to English forts built 1548–50 in Scotland, concluding that references to the 'King's Work' at this Cork Harbor site indicate that its construction had begun under Edward VI.

30 This construction, if not composite, looks more like a siege or field camp than a fort.

31 Kerrigan, *Castles and Fortifications*, p. 56, notes that it was nearly finished in August 1602.

32 Evidence for a round flanker at the southeast corner of James Fort in Virginia has been revealed by archaeology. See W. M. Kelso, *Jamestown, The Buried Truth* (Charlottesville and London, 2006), pp. 58–66, where it is also suggested that the bastion was soon converted to a demilune form, containing a small sunken magazine.

33 The influence of the Dutch war on tactics was great, as shown for example in Robert Norton, *The ... Practise of Artillerie* (London, 1628), and Col. Henry Gage, *The Siege of Breda* (London, 1627). Rouse, *Expansion of Elizabethan England*, pp. 415–16, and Falls, *Elizabeth's Irish Wars*, p. 10, agree that England had to employ its best generals in Ireland, and that the sheer misery of campaign conditions led to Sir William Pelham's contemporary claim: 'all the soldiers in Christendom must give place in that to the soldier of Ireland'. I would thus consider the Irish wars to be one stage in a military evolution that began in the mid-sixteenth-century Scottish campaigns, grew in the Netherlands, and saw its culmination in the changes noted in Rolf Loeber and Geoffrey Parker, 'The military revolution in seventeenth century Ireland', in Ohlmeyer (ed.), *Ireland from Independence to Occupation*, pp. 66–88.

3

Colonial settlement

For, indeed, what hope was there that a sort of husbandmen trained up in peace, placed abroad in sundry places, dispersed as your land lay dispersed, should be able to maintain and defend themselves against a people newly recovered out of the relics of rebellion, and yet practicing arms and warlike exercises?

Edmund Spenser, 1598[1]

The 1500s saw the Hapsburg Empire spreading across the globe and Valois France claiming supremacy as the most populous and prosperous nation in Europe. Tudor England, however, retained only remnants of its medieval domains. On the Continent, the Plantagenet legacy was reduced to a small zone defending Calais. Hegemony over the Scots was a thing of the past. Authority in Ireland had shrunk to the walled cities and the fifty-mile-wide Pale around Dublin.[2] French royal power pressed upon the Tudors at Calais, but in Ireland and along the Scottish border, English rule was challenged and essentially neutralized by the 'feudal anarchy' of a resurgent Celtic aristocracy. International politics, religious conflicts, and succession problems deflected Henry VIII's natural tendency toward expansionism, but by 1540, near the end of his reign, he was prepared for further English aggrandizement. By 1640, the course of English overseas colonization was set. This first century of tentative and uncoordinated efforts would see the English becoming masters of a territorial and commercial empire that stretched from a united British archipelago to possessions in North America, the Caribbean, and even India.[3]

This chapter considers the context of Elizabethan settlement in Ireland by examining the forms of early English colonization: the physical structure of settlements, the activities taking place within them, and the functions these sites fulfilled. The first hundred years of proto-colonial activities divide historically into thirds. The first period (1540–75) witnessed Protector Somerset's aggressive moves in Ireland

and Scotland, Mary's unwise entanglement in Hapsburg policy and the subsequent loss of Calais, and Elizabeth's venturing beyond the cautious, county-building Irish policy of her predecessor to approve several overly ambitious private colonies that not only failed to take root, but further antagonized the Irish. The second phase (1575–1606) began with the rebellion and confiscatory defeat of the Earl of Desmond, which enabled the Privy Council to distribute about one fourth of the Munster province among courtiers and investors. This phase continued with a series of unsuccessful royally approved attempts to establish a foothold on the North American coast and ended with the destruction of both the Munster Plantation and the Irish forces of resistance. The final period (1606–40) saw several major developments: the resettlement of pacified Munster; the flight of the 'Wild Geese' earls and their supporters from Ulster; and the distribution of their lands to London guild companies and the planting there of settlers from Scotland and north England. At the same time, efforts to colonize North America were renewed with the chartering of the Virginia and Plymouth Companies, later transformed into colonial administrations. The proto-colonial century concluded with the interruption of effective state-directed colonization, as the unity of the British Isles, and of England itself, dissolved in the overlapping conflicts of the Civil War.[4]

Sources and methods for settlement analysis

The character of colonization is intimately associated with the types of settlements planned, attempted, and successfully established. The origins of such settlement planning, on each side of the British Atlantic, were first explored thirty years ago in Maurice Beresford's *New Towns of the Middle Ages* and in John Reps's *Tidewater Towns*. Examining the period between the two studies, David Quinn was simultaneously, in many authoritative works, bringing to light details of Elizabethan efforts to colonize Ireland and America.[5]

These three major contributors to English proto-colonial studies used sources provided by documentary and cartographic archives, but they would also adopt methodologies employed by historical geographers. In Ireland, more recent historical research on the colonial settlements, starting with Nicholas Canny's *Elizabethan Conquest of Ireland*, has been supplemented by efforts of historical geographers such as John Andrews and Rolf Loeber, as well as growing numbers of archaeologists.[6]

In the 1950s, the American colonies supplied archaeological evidence from such sites as Jamestown and Roanoke to supplement poorly documented histories. In the ensuing generation, what is called 'historical archaeology' in America and 'post-medieval archaeology' in Europe matured as a discipline, as the experience of hundreds of sites produced a broader and more reliable set of data for the material culture of the early modern British Isles and its overseas offshoots. This in turn has recently sparked renewed interest in the proto-colonial period. Fieldwork at Frobisher's Bay on Baffin Island; Roanoke Island in North Carolina; Jamestown, Virginia; and St Mary's City, Maryland begin to offer dramatic reinterpretations of the archaeological and historical record.[7]

Although sometimes misused, the 'hard facts' of archaeology serve as valuable checks on the often insufficient or conflicting documentary, cartographic, and oral traditions. Certain aspects of archaeological stratigraphy are indisputable, in that the record can be destroyed or obscured, but cannot be false, provided enough context for comparison within the site and among similar sites. Archaeological fieldwork is also an important source of new primary data for early colonization. For instance, while many early seventeenth-century sites in the Chesapeake Tidewater have identifiable landowners, the name and history of the tenants or servants who actually occupied most of these sites are unknown. Yet the scores of small farms now located and the discernible patterns they formed of settlement at different times in the seventeenth century provide a new context for re-examining the documentary histories.

The study of proto-colonial settlement has largely focused on evidence for town planning and a search for models, either created by Elizabethan minds addressing the problems of settlement, or based on examples drawn from Classical literature or earlier Renaissance colonizing projects. How important, though, was this planning and those models, especially to the colonists themselves?

Periods of settlement

1540–75

The first period of English proto-colonial settlement (essentially early Tudor) employed two types of colonial projects: first, the royally initiated government operations of Henry, Edward, and Mary; and later, the royally chartered private projects of Elizabeth. The earlier settlements were related to broader considerations of strategic defence and may be considered as much an element of frontier defence-in-depth as colonization. Thus, these plantations should be considered in the context of such

Tudor projects as Henry VIII's system of coastal artillery defences or the fortifications at Berwick, Hull, Plymouth, and even Tilbury.[8]

The earliest settlement project was that drawn up by Henry himself in 1540, as part of a major effort to fortify the marches of the Calais Pale, the 20-mile-wide territory around England's last continental possession (see Figure 3.1). A survey of 1540 proposed six new bulwarks and a 28-foot-wide dyke to guard the eastern zone, in the marshes across from the French-held town of Ardres. In addition, a drawing shows a planned settlement as an irregular rectilinear shape designed to fit the topography and defensive needs. It was to comprise seventy-six houses dispersed at set intervals, each with as much as fifty acres of attached agricultural lands. Defence was to be based upon a centrally placed, fortified church, but plans for the settlement seem to have been dropped, because construction of only the bulwarks and dykes was undertaken in 1541 and completed by 1545.[9]

Henry's policies continued westward expansion after his death. The Anglo-Irish merchant class that dominated the Dublin Pale had

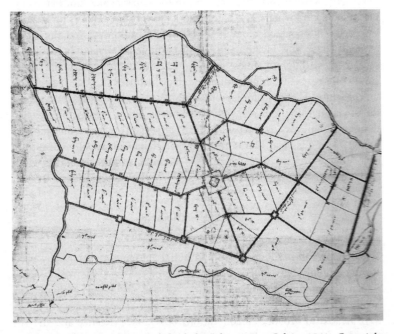

Figure 3.1 Plan of projected defended settlement at Calais, 1541. Copyright British Library Board: BL Cotton MS Augustus I. ii. 69.

convinced Henry in 1540 that the failure to control unruly native lords could be remedied only by a major constitutional change: Ireland's conversion from a lordship to a kingdom. The new king of Ireland would hold title to several monarchies (England, France, and Ireland), and thus could claim an imperial status equal to his great rivals Charles V and Francis I. In Ireland, the authority of the Dublin Parliament was now theoretically equal to that of the English Parliament, and the merchant class could run the affairs of state more to their liking – and less to that of the aristocracy. Defending the Pale by building new forts and planting settlements to support the garrisons came next. As noted in previous chapters, Forts Governor and Protector were constructed during Edward VI's reign in the disputed lands along the watershed between the Pale and the Shannon valley. Under Mary, settlements associated with these forts were given the name Maryborough and Philipstown. They soon received charters and borough status, becoming the county seats for the newly created King's and Queen's Counties (Offaly and Laois). Surviving maps indicate that the towns were laid out on a simple grid, surrounded by a rectangular wall or earthwork that tied into the defensive line of the fort (see below). The towns were never very populous, nor did their forts play decisive roles in the wars to come, but that might also be a measure of their success. These sites were not abandoned in the Elizabethan Wars that followed; the two towns retained their occupants and the forts their garrisons.

Other projects proved less successful. In the barony of Kerrycurrihy not far from Cork City, Sir Warham St Leger obtained lands as debt compensation from the Earl of Desmond. He tried to secure the estate and its rentals by planting a number of Englishmen there, along with members of his own family. It seems to have been an example of a military-ruled native settlement, administered and defended from Tracton Abbey and Carrigaline Castle, which were attacked in a provincial uprising. The 1569 assault on both castle and abbey and the death of the occupants were heavy blows to those English interested in development and colonization in Munster. At the other end of the island, Ulster, where Elizabeth's government was essentially powerless, was now the subject of several colonizing efforts. Garrison towns were established at Newry, Carrickfergus, and Coleraine. The statesman Sir Thomas Smith, thinking along Classical lines, proposed that English settlements in Ulster were the most suitable answer to both the unmanageable northern lordships and the threat of Scottish migration. The best known of these ventures was that undertaken by Smith himself on the strategic Ards peninsula. Seen as a base from which to spread English control up the Antrim coast, this colony, to have a capital city named 'Elizabetha', was funded by public subscription. Here, too, such efforts were seen to threaten the existing (dis)order. The authorities in Dublin did little to help the fledgling settlement (probably a defended village), and in 1575 it was destroyed in an attack following the murder of its governor, Smith's own son. Ulster remained the target of Elizabethan colonial entrepreneurs. Soon Walter Devereau, Earl of Essex, used his personal fortune to set up a colony, but this in turn failed due to overly optimistic planning, an uncooperative provincial government, and an antagonistic native population.[10]

The first period of English overseas colonization was one of much trial and more error. It witnessed the final failure in France, and the modest success of garrisoned county towns in Ireland was matched by the squandered treasure and lives that private colonies lost there. But a third area was quietly flourishing. English fishing fleets from Bristol and elsewhere had been drawing upon an inexhaustible supply of fish in the Grand Banks and Gulf of St Laurence. The most profitable arrangement was to spend the summer on Newfoundland, drying, salting, or smoking the catches, and return in the autumn laden with fish preserved for use the rest of the year. These independent, seasonally occupied settlements developed organically, without directive from government and perhaps even guild. It also seems that foreign fishermen acted with the same freedom, and this broadly 'European' enterprise worked amicably, for the profit of all concerned.

1576–1605

England's second generation of expansion shifted farther westward. Activity occurred again in Ireland but not in France. More concrete colonies appeared in North America, and there was even a South American venture. Private settlements continued to be proposed as a profitable way to stabilize areas of the Irish countryside, but Elizabeth was no longer receptive to them. The Privy Council chose to avoid both the expenses of state colonization and the lack of control evident in private colonies when it created a hybrid form, the Munster Plantation (see Figure 3.2). There, the Earl of Desmond's escheated land holdings were divided into 'seignories' of 12,000 potentially arable acres, and long leases were given to men of substance who showed themselves fit to raise the number of tenant settlers and the necessary capital improvements of house building, fencing, ditching, etc., required by the leases. The government created the plan for colonization and would hope to benefit from loyal subjects,

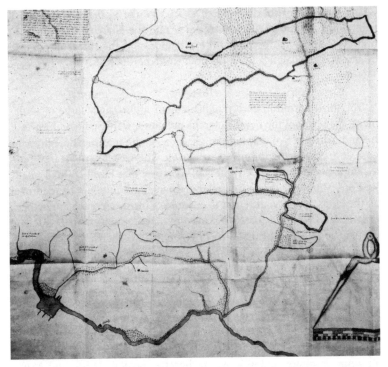

Figure 3.2 Contemporary map of the land survey for Raleigh's estates along the Blackwater River.

improved defence forces, and eventually income from leases and markets, but was spared the administration of the actual settlement process.

Despite its plausibility, this new scheme, which went into effect in 1586, failed its original participants after a dozen years. In 1598, the Earl of Tyrone's longstanding rebellion in Ulster spread rapidly into Munster, with a widespread uprising that soon left only four places under English control outside the medieval walled towns. At Mogeely Castle (see below), colonists had erected half-timbered dwellings in several locales: the partially nucleated settlement with a central green between castle and church; the new, rectilinear undefended settlement of Curraglass; and several isolated farmsteads. Throughout Munster, English landowners often occupied the small, late medieval 'tower-house' castles commonly at the centres of major manors, sometimes reconstructing them to fit Renaissance or chivalric ideals. Yet the assault came swiftly, without warning, and was often carried by neighbours and servants. Mogeely

Castle was one of the few places to survive the uprising, but English habitations around it were destroyed. Amid the anarchy of subsequent military campaigns to control the province, and the threat of Spanish intervention, Raleigh sold off his now-ruined properties.

1606–40

The third period of early English colonization saw a surge of settlement, the result of the new monarch's policies toward Spain and towards Ireland, which a Scottish king might view as the traditional, legitimate, goal of Scottish emigration or expansion. The Ulster lords feared both his duplicity and the effectiveness of the army that Elizabeth had finally let Lord Mountjoy create for Ireland. Their flight in effect handed over all the lands James would need to ensure a Scottish presence in northern Ireland, and he soon forced his new, moneyed, subjects in London to participate in a new programme of colonization. The Ulster settlements belonged to several types (defended and undefended villages, dispersed defended farms, and military occupied native structures), the strongest motive for which was immigration.

In North America, the fragile colonial settlements of the early seventeenth century avoided extermination less by Spanish impotence than by the Hapsburgs' diplomatic need to detach James from his family's traditional ally, France. Thus the principal fort and accompanying town in Virginia (Jamestown, 1607), Massachusetts (Boston, 1630), and Maryland (St Mary's, 1634) served as nuclei of three rapidly growing colonies. In all three, elements of fortification in settlements were abandoned as the frontier moved westward. Elsewhere, the many forts of early Bermuda (1611) speak more of its position on the route of the Spanish Plate Fleet than to a settlement scheme. English settlers in the Caribbean proper, starting with St Kitts in 1624 and Barbados in 1627, faced greater dangers: the Carib natives, other colonizing European nations, and (especially after Raleigh's abortive and bloody 1618 campaign in Guiana) the Spanish Empire, which, unable to settle all the islands it claimed, nevertheless succeeded in destroying competing settlements. Many seem to have combined a fort-and-town with dispersed settlements, but for this subject there is little documentary evidence, and less archaeology.

Elizabethan settlement in Ireland

Queen Elizabeth threw open in 1584 to English colonization in Munster the vast but scattered estates of the attainted Earl of Desmond, but little written evidence describes how the new colonial communities were established and what physical layout they were given.[11] This lack of documentation and the piecemeal nature of the Munster Plantation could lead one to assume that the new settlements were unplanned, haphazard affairs. Yet other early English colonizing ventures are seen to display a strong interest in urbanism. In writing about the Ulster plantations, R. H. Buchanan referred to the establishment of towns as 'the most significant and enduring contribution of the English plantations, in Ireland as well as overseas,' and Philip Robinson asserted that 'the concept of urban living was central to English plantation theory.'[12] The collapse of the Munster plantation in 1598, and indeed the general failure of Elizabethan colonies in contrast to the general success of Stuart plantations, could well be related to a lack of settlement planning. But evidence does exist – both cartographic and archaeological – for new settlements of regular design, which would place planned towns and villages in Elizabethan Munster a generation before the colonies of Ulster and Virginia.

We have seen how Tudor interest in colonizing Ireland began with Edward VI and Mary, who undertook to defend the Dublin Pale by a forward chain of military outposts similar to the English enclave of Calais.[13] Two forts, Protector and Governor, were constructed in Edward's reign, and under Mary, English people were planted in the districts that became Queen's County and King's County. At a time when the English court felt the influence of Spain and its imperial practices, it is perhaps not uncoincidental that towns – Philipstown and Maryborough – were created at the forts (see Figure 3. 3) Indeed, David Quinn considered the towns examples of a 'Spanish' colonial policy promoted by Sir Henry Sidney and Sir Thomas Smith.[14] The royal garrisons stimulated the local economies, and both settlements prospered, becoming market towns in 1567 and boroughs in 1569.[15]

Mary's planting of English people in Laois and Offaly and the extension of traditional English county government to those districts heralded many schemes for Irish colonization. Few received official approval. Of those, only a handful actually entered the settlement process. Despite the Court connections of such leaders as Sir Richard Grenville, Sir Warham St Leger, and Sir Thomas Smith, the communities they managed to establish around 1570 soon failed. If the small size of the plantations and the difficulty in raising piecemeal capital and colonists were the cause of failure, this would be corrected by the next effort in Irish colonization. The Earl of Desmond's death in 1583 ended the rebellion he had begun in 1579, and his escheated lands were divided into 'signories' of

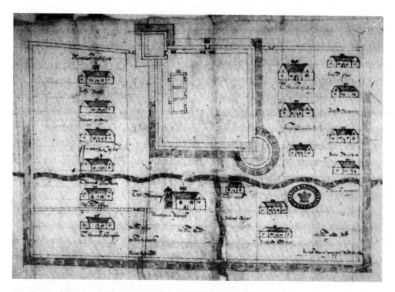

Figure 3.3 Map of Maryborough, sixteenth century.

12,000 acres. The infant colony took form in 1586 when parties began to survey the escheated lands for the new grantees. Sir Walter Raleigh's courtesies to the queen were rewarded; Elizabeth gave him alone 40,000 acres, apparently most of the Desmond holdings along the rivers Blackwater and Bride. He and other grantees were less successful in replacing the Irish with English farmers and artisans than in exploiting the natural resources, especially timber, in an especially aggressive manner. Twelve years of sullen acquiescence in Munster suddenly ended with the native Irish uprising of October 1598, which rapidly destroyed the English colonial establishment throughout Munster.

Following the English victory at Kinsale in 1601, the colonization of Munster could resume. But many landholders did not carry over into the new reign. Edmund Spenser died soon after fleeing Kilcolman Castle, and as E. P. Cheney put it, 'Raleigh disposed of his grant in disgust.'[16] Sir Richard Boyle, secretary of the Munster Council and a political ally of the Lord President, Sir George Carew, seized this and other opportunities to amass the largest accumulation of landholdings in Munster. It was under the leadership of Boyle, later to become 'The Great Earl of Cork', that the second plantation of Munster took place. This development was made easier because of the failure of Tyrone's rebellion, and the Spanish intervention eliminated all opposition to the English and their

Irish allies, especially in Munster. With some justification, the original scheme for settlement was thought unreliable, and the standard 12,000 acre seigneury was abandoned.

The death of Elizabeth and surrender of Tyrone in 1603 witnessed a few years of quiet during which the Stuart succession removed the only source of effective support for Irish autonomy, let alone independence. The Flight of the Earls from James's avarice and treachery, however, generated a colonization effort on an even greater scale. Beginning in 1610, new settlements spread throughout the province of Ulster. Urbanism was an important element of the plan, which was carried out by companies of capital investment drawn from the London guilds. The City's wealth ensured that an important strategic position translated into economic and urban growth for (London)Derry. Other towns less fortunate prospered nonetheless. By 1620, there were several corporate towns in Ulster, and many market towns. Colonists from England, Wales and Scotland poured into the north, and soon created stable communities that replaced the indigenous population.[17]

Was the model of urbanism the key to colonization in Ireland? Even if the first-period Philipstown and Maryborough did not develop into great urban centres, neither did they fail. They and the counties they served endured the warfare of the late sixteenth century. In an early scheme for colonizing Ulster, Sir Thomas Smith had hoped to establish the city of Elizabetha in the Ards. If planned towns contributed to the successful planting of Laois, Offaly, and eventually Ulster, it could be argued that the Elizabethan failure in Munster should be attributed to a lack of planned settlements.[18]

But recognizing the advantages of urbanism is not the same as adhering to the Renaissance aesthetic principle of spatial regularity. In the absence of sufficient documentary evidence to comment confidently, one must turn to archaeology. Despite Ireland's distance from the main currents of the Renaissance, the Elizabethan wars caused traditional forms to be replaced by Renaissance designs. We have seen in Chapter 2 that at Dunboy Castle, the last Munster stronghold to fall to Elizabeth's armies, the tower-keep and bawn enclosure were replaced in 1602 by new defences incorporating elements of symmetry and angled bastions.[19] That Renaissance fort was designed by Spanish expeditionary forces or by Irish officers experienced in the French Wars of Religion, demonstrating that even the enemies of the Tudor plantations brought Renaissance planning with them. As in the Netherlands, English armies in Ireland employed regular designs for encampments and fortifications.[20]

The martial background of most English leaders of the Munster colony implies a receptivity to – or predilection for – such planning, which could appear as readily in civil as in military undertakings. Urban planning was part of English proto-colonial thinking. *The Jewell of Artes*, George Waymouth's attempt to persuade the newly crowned James to search for the Northwest Passage, contained a treatise on the planning and defence of colonial towns, which was accompanied by imaginatively symmetrical plans for fortified towns.[21]

Tudor colonization in Ireland embraced, first, the principles of planning and regularity implicit in Elizabethan military tactics and construction, and second, the directed urbanism that created Maryborough, Philipstown, and even Elizabetha. But can one then infer planned settlements in Munster, which already had several rich Anglo-Irish cities and many flourishing native communities outside the escheated Desmond lands? The evidence against planned settlements in Munster is strong. Immediately after the 1598 uprising William Saxey, Chief Justice of Munster, wrote that a successful plantation *would have* comprised communities of at least twenty households enclosed by a defensive ditch.[22] Such settlements would have been fair-sized villages, and could arguably have served as the basis for developing towns. But Saxey's point was that these ideal settlements never materialized. Too few colonists was offered by another contemporary, Fynes Moryson, as the cause of failure: 'For whereas they should have built Castles, and brought over Colonies from England, and have admitted no Irish Tenant but onely English, these and like covenants were in no part performed by them'. [23]

Yet Renaissance schemes did exist for the colony's rational organization. A proposal made in 1585 for the settlement of Munster contained a scheme for uniform administrative districts. The idea was to establish 'hundreds' – judicial and taxing divisions of a county or shire. The Irish hundred was to comprise nine parishes, eight agricultural parishes surrounding one with a country town.[24] Each parish was to contain 108 families, and therefore 972 families per hundred, or very roughly 4000 English per hundred. This scheme for colonization would never have succeeded, given the conditions in Munster. First, the scattered tracts of escheated Desmond lands simply could not have provided, as a norm, the space for eight agricultural parishes around a commercial centre. Second, migration to Munster never grew large enough to support numbers such as 108 families per parish; it perhaps reached only one-tenth that amount. The population for a single hundred in the proposal nearly matches what has been estimated for all the English colonists in Munster.[25] The historical geographer, John Andrews, points to the dispersed settlement pattern that proved functional for Ireland's agricultural communities, contrasted with the nucleated settlements of the English colonists: 'the townland's success was the plantation's failure'.[26]

When active colonization began in 1586, the hundred scheme was not followed, but there is evidence that nucleated communities were considered the basis of settlement. Sir Walter Raleigh's newly planted tenants at Moghelly [*sic*], in eastern County Cork, were given specific orders to 'dwell in the town ... keep their arms in readiness ... [and] ... all upon the sound of the drum repair to the castle gate'.[27] The instructions do not describe the layout of the settlement, but they clearly concern a nucleated 'town' site adjacent to Mogeely Castle. The question is, did this prescription for a kind of structured community translate into a layout of planned regularity? The answer appears some years later, when the Mogeely estate was leased by Raleigh to his business associate, Henry Pyne. The only surviving estate map of sixteenth-century Ireland, a map drawn in 1598 to accompany Pyne's lease (or its confirmation) reveals the degree to which the orders for the Mogeely settlers had been obeyed in the ensuing twelve years[28] (see Figure 3. 4) Archaeological fieldwork in 1990–92 checked the map's accuracy.[29] Distances between surviving landmarks were found to match those of the map. Test excavation and geophysical survey corroborated other details by finding evidence of the rectangular mortared stone foundation of a colonial house. The map reveals that in 1598, a nucleated settlement did exist, but in a state of incompletion. New fields had been laid out and fenced, and Pyne spanned the diminutive River Bride by an impressive stone bridge, which may indeed be still standing (see Figure 3.5). Outside the castle gate lay an open area, perhaps a new village green or town square, but most likely based upon the previous forecourt or outer bailey of the castle (see Figure 3.6). Several English-style houses of timber frame construction flanked the 'green' and the road leading south. Others were scattered throughout the neighbourhood.

Three observations can be made about Elizabethan Mogeely. (1) The English houses (outbuildings were omitted) were sited on a regular spacing and orientation. They flanked the road but did not lie haphazardly along it, as in contemporary depictions of northern European villages. (2) Much of the town was still unoccupied, yet several houses were squeezed in awkwardly between the church and the street in front of it. This suggests that land formerly pertaining to the church had been given over to other purposes, but whether this was done by Raleigh, Pyne,

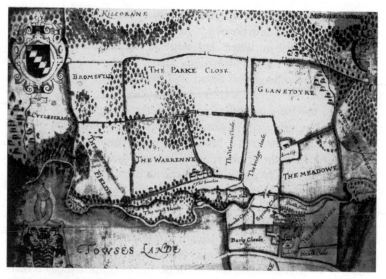

Figure 3.4 Mogeely Estate Map, northwest and centre, 1598.

or even the town clerk, Alexander Stynte, is not known.[30] (3) The placement of the house sites in such close proximity is striking, given the large
amount of unoccupied land. The individual lots therefore must have been
relatively small. In 1615, the standard lot in the English redevelopment of
the Ulster town of Armagh measured fifty feet by one hundred fifty feet.[31]
The excavations at Wolstenholme Towne in Martin's Hundred in Virginia
revealed that the town, occupied from 1619 to 1622, was divided into
properties with frontages at multiples of approximately forty-five feet.[32]
The Mogeely house lots may have had similar dimensions.

One can conclude that in 1598 Mogeely was an embryonic – perhaps
stillborn – nucleated community. If Raleigh had hoped to duplicate his
property in Dorset, where the town of Sherborne prospered beside Sherborne Castle, he was disappointed. What population there was by Mogeely
Castle had built traditional English houses, set on a regular alignment in
house plots about fifty feet wide. Raleigh's map shows why the town had
not developed sufficiently. More English settlers lived in the countryside
around Mogeely than in the town. Their houses joined and sometimes
replaced the native Irish huts or cabins that lay scattered among several
hamlets in the Mogeely area (see Figures 1.9, 3.7). The 1992–93 excavations of the Carrigeen settlement, northwest of Mogeely Castle, suggested
a short-lived English occupation of a pre-existing Irish *clachan* hamlet.[33]

Figure 3.5 Mogeely Bridge with castle in background, from the northwest.

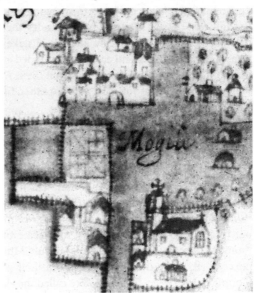

Figure 3.6 Mogeely village and castle. Detail of Mogeely Estate Map.

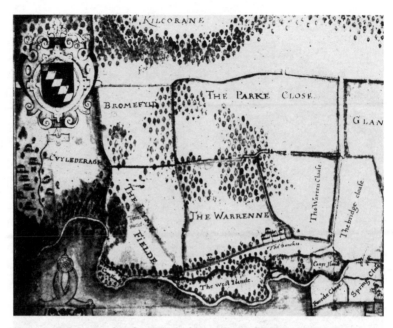

Figure 3.7 Carrigeen hamlet. Detail of Mogeely Estate Map.

This remarkable map, designed to show the holdings of the tenants that Raleigh was passing on to Pyne, illustrates the failure of the courtier's colonial settlement at Mogeely, and the mistakes of the Munster Plantation as a whole. These mistakes certainly led to the colony's failure to defend itself in the uprising of October 1598. Although Mogeely Castle managed to hold out for Pyne, all the other English houses and lands were lost for miles around.[34]

The same map depicts a portion of the neighbouring manor of Curraglass (see Figure 3.8). It was part of Raleigh's vast estate, but was not included in the lease of lands around Mogeely Castle. The settlement was a new foundation and was destroyed in the revolt, like Tallow, its neighbour just across the Waterford border, which was reported to have held 120 'able bodied men, all English'.[35] Little is known about Curraglass, but its inhabitants did have one claim to fame – or infamy. They were singled out in a report to London as the worst case of litigiousness and acrimonious behaviour in the generally unruly Munster colony. 'They were never quiet, while they had a penny in their purses, but arresting and binding to the peace, that they were called the clampers of Curryglasse'.[36]

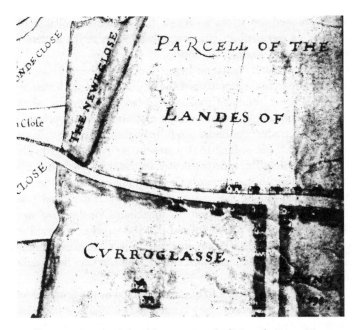

Figure 3.8 Curraglass English settlement. Detail of Mogeely Estate Map.

Their private lives or business affairs may have been contentious, but their community as seen on the Mogeely map and confirmed by surviving boundaries was laid out with regularity, not a linear street village, but a cross-roads (or T-junction) settlement. The houses follow a single alignment, and one may assume that the plots were of standard size, interspersed with undeveloped properties. Here too, some English houses, perhaps those of the more prosperous tenants, were located outside the village, apparently on their own landholdings.

Corroborated by archaeology, the Raleigh map reveals the strengths and weaknesses of Elizabethan colonial settlement in Ireland. It depicts one nucleated community, one quasi-nucleated, several hamlets with houses of both Irish and English style, and some isolated English farmhouses. Raleigh's instructions refer to Mogeely as a town, but it certainly developed less than he intended. Many of the English on the Mogeely estate preferred to live in dispersed *clachan* hamlets. A more successful nucleated English settlement was Curraglass, though even here some of the settlers lived in isolated farmhouses. The 1586 Munster colony did plan and create regular towns and villages, but the forces for dispersed settlement proved too strong to resist. The immediate collapse of the colony in 1598 was attributed quite rightly by Saxey to the settlers' typically dispersed and unprotected houses.

A second Munster Plantation began soon after the 1601 victory at Kinsale and once again emphasized the advantages of nucleated settlement. In 1605, Sir Thomas Crooke leased land at Baltimore where he established a community that thrived on southwest Ireland's privateering and smuggling trade.[37] Baltimore was fully English, receiving its borough charter in 1612.[38] But in June 1631 it was the scene of a tragedy unique to the British Isles. The little town was assaulted by Turkish Janissary soldiers and Moorish and renegade Christian sailors, sent by the Pashaw of Algiers.[39] Led by one Jan Jansen, who had taken the Turkish name of Morat Rais, the Muslims seized 107 inhabitants for the slave markets of North Africa. It was not unnoticed that the target of this raid was a new settlement of English Protestants, and in fact, the slavers had been directed there by an Irishman, one Hackett, who was later hanged for his actions.

Richard Boyle, the Great Earl of Cork, alarmed by the general Muslim threat to the Munster coast, sent a crudely drawn 'mapp of the Harbour and Towne of Baltimore,' to Lord Dorchester, the Secretary of State[40] (see Figure 1.11). The accompanying letter noted that the map showed how easily Baltimore Harbour could be defended. Its date of 19 February 1631 would have followed the old tradition of starting the year in March, so the corrected 1632 date is a case of hindsight and rumor (the Algerians never did return) instead of foresight and warning.[41] The Boyle map depicts two settlements at Baltimore Harbour, the little fishing village called the Cove and the town of Baltimore itself. E. J. Priestly, who discovered the map, observed that 'the regular layout of the houses near the castle to its west, north and east suggests they comprise the planned recent English settlement, while the less regular layout of the houses south of the castle would seem to show that these comprise the village that existed prior to the establishment of the English settlement'.[42] Priestly could be right, but the layout of houses south of the castle seems little different from the others, and it is likely that all represent the new town of the seventeenth century.

Few if any original buildings have survived at Baltimore. After the Algerian attack, the town declined and had little population until recent times. The details of the Boyle map can be related to the topography of modern Baltimore. The castle, comprising a fortified house and enclosure wall, stands upon a outcrop that joins the town at the northeast. From that point, streets descend steeply south to the quayside and west to an area totally altered by the erection of an eighteenth-century mansion and a nineteenth-century fish-packing plant and rail terminal. At the base of the cliff face to the south, however, one can find indications of rock cuttings for the early seventeenth-century houses.[43]

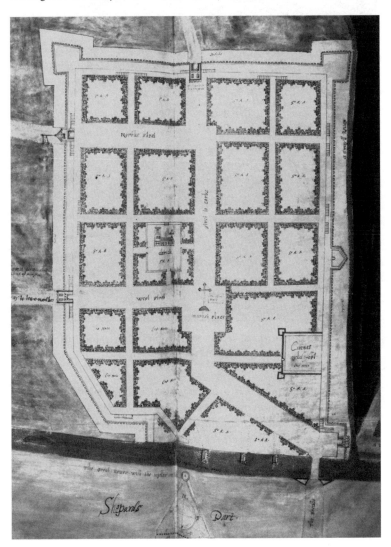

Figure 3.9 Early seventeenth-century map of Bandon, Co. Cork. The northwest gate bears the initials 'RB' for Richard Boyle, and a flag with '1613' upon it.

Figure 3.10 North transept of seventeenth-century Christchurch, Bandon. The change in masonry marks the original roof line.

Plantation Baltimore was a densely occupied, nucleated settlement, forthrightly rectilinear in plan. The town had five streets, and at the intersection of the two roads leading out of town, a square or green (where the name 'Baltimore' is written on the map) faced what most likely was the castle entrance. The map shows forty-six houses in the town of Baltimore itself; the Algerians broke into forty houses before they withdrew. Outside the town proper were fishermen's homes scattered along the shore from the castle rock to the cove. The first targets of the Algerian attack, these probably represent the original settlement, from which the Irish natives had fled or been expelled after the rebellion collapsed at Kinsale. Thirty years later, with the second Munster Plantation well established, most of Baltimore's English population was taken off to permanent captivity –

only a handful ever returned. English Baltimore was destroyed by proxy, and the native Irish of Munster may well have felt revenged for their losses.

A well-known early seventeenth-century documentary source supplements the evidence for settlement planning from these archaeological and cartographic sources, and displays the contemporary association – or competition – between Munster and Ulster. Sir Richard Boyle purchased and expanded the settlement of Bandonbridge by duplication on either side of the River Bandon (see Figure 3.9). In what his biographer called 'a testament of achievement,' Boyle wrote: 'My new town of Bandon is more in compass than Londonderry, that my walls are stronger thicker higher than theirs, only they have a stronger rampier within. ... In my town there is built a strong bridge over the river, two large session houses, two market houses, with two fair churches.'[44]

The bridge, walls, civic buildings, and one of the churches of Bandon were replaced long ago. Christ Church still stands and may be the earliest surviving church of the Munster Plantation. It was erected in 1610 apparently as a cruciform structure thirty feet (10m) wide by at least sixty feet (20m) long, with transepts twenty-four feet (8m) square (see Figure 3.10). The success of Boyle's 'new town of Bandon' led to a porch addition in 1629, and the nave walls were raised and the bell tower altered in the early eighteenth century. But with the waning of English influence in Ireland, and in the absence of a viable congregation, Christ Church was deconsecrated in the late 1900s and, after some years of decay, it came to serve as a community heritage centre. Not enough comparative structures are known from Munster to judge its typicality as a Plantation church. One should note, however, that many Ulster Plantation churches were built without transepts, as were the earliest colonial churches of Virginia, though others were cruciform. The transepts may simply reflect the size of the congregation.

Magnates like Boyle and planters like Sir Thomas Crooke understood the strategic necessity of establishing reliable population centres at important harbours, river crossings, and mountainous areas. They also saw the economic necessity of rapidly exploiting the natural resources of Munster to make such settlements profitable and secure. In both plantation periods, Munster may have offered fewer opportunities for adventurers than Ulster or America. The continued presence of Irish and Old English in Munster always confined the Elizabethan plantations spatially and legally, and interest, investment, and ultimately population would flow elsewhere. Jacobean colonists in Ulster and America would successfully establish planned towns and villages, but such communities could also be found in Munster a generation earlier. From Spenser's isolated castle to Raleigh's wholesale adoption of – and by – the port town of Youghal, the English chose various forms of settlement, including planned communities, though few would last. For a brief period, Elizabeth's councillors and courtiers believed that the ambition and rationality of Renaissance England could produce effortless expansion. The Munster Plantation was in fact a 'paper state', a settlement of great expectations only. Like the other scenes of Tudor expansion, Elizabethan Ireland witnessed colonialism without colonization.

Notes

1 *State Papers* [Ireland] 188, No. 18, quoted on p. 269 in R. Dunlop, 'The plantation of Munster, 1584–1589', *English Hist. Rev.* 3 (1888), pp. 250–69. See also R. Gottfried, *Spenser's Prose Works* (Baltimore, 1949), 'A Brief Note of Ireland', p. 238.

2 Yet these towns served as the core of future developments. R. A. Butlin, asserts: 'In a sense, the urban system of [Elizabethan] Ireland at this time formed part of an imperial system, based on England', p. 157 in 'Land and people, c. 1600', in T. W. Moody, F. X. Martin, and F. J. Byrne (eds), *A New History of Ireland* (Oxford, 1976), pp. 142–67.

3 The Tudor shift from relative isolation to cautious – then aggressive – expansionism is imaginatively treated in A. L. Rowse, *The Expansion of Elizabethan England* (London, 1955). Some followed on a similarly large but different canvas, e.g., T. O. Lloyd, *The British Empire 1558–1983* (Oxford, 1984). Others were more focused: D. B. Quinn, *Raleigh and the British Empire* (London, 1947), *The Roanoke Voyages, 1584–1590* (London, 1955), and *The Elizabethans in Ireland* (Ithaca, 1966); G. V. Scammell, *The World Encompassed. The First European Maritime Empires c. 800–1650* (Berkeley, 1981), pp. 458–503; and K. R. Andrews, *Trade, Plunder and Settlement: Maritime Enterprise and the Genesis of the British Empire, 1480–1630* (Cambridge, 1984). More recently, Nicholas Canny *et al.* have treated the subject topically in *The Origins of Empire: British Overseas Enterprise to the Close of the Seventeenth Century. Vol I, The Oxford History of the British Empire* (Oxford, 1998), especially N. Canny, 'The origins of empire: An introduction', pp. 1–33.

4 The stages in the relationship between the English Crown and its Irish dominion during this 'proto-colonial century' bear comparison to the periods of denominational relations proposed by Ute Lotz-Huemann, 'Confessionalism in Ireland: Periodisation and character', in Alan Ford and John McCafferty (eds), *The Origins of Sectarianism in Early Modern Ireland* (Cambridge, 2005), pp. 24–53.

5 See M. Beresford, *New Towns of the Middle Ages: Town Plantation in England, Wales and Gascony* (London, 1967); J. Reps, *Tidewater Towns: City Planning in Colonial Virginia and Maryland* (1972); and D. B. Quinn *The Voyages and Colonizing Enterprises of Sir Humphrey Gilbert* (London, 1940), as well as the encyclopedic compilation, with A. M. Quinn and S. Hillier (eds), *New American World: A Documentary History of North America to 1612* (New York, 1979).

6 N. Canny, *The Elizabethan Conquest of Ireland* (Hassocks, Sussex, 1976); J. Andrews, *Irish Maps* (Sussex, New York, 1985); R. Loeber, *The Geography and Practice of English Colonization in Ireland* (Athlone, 1991); D. Power, 'The archaeology of the Munster Plantation', pp.197–201 in M. Ryan (ed.), *The Illustrated Archaeology of Ireland* (Dublin, 1991); and E. Klingelhofer, 'Proto-colonial archaeology: the case of Elizabethan Ireland',

in P. Funari, M. Hall, and S. Jones (eds), *Back from the Edge: Archaeology in History* (London, 1999), pp. 164–79.

7 W. A. Kenyon, *Tokens of Possession: The Northern Voyages of Martin Frobisher* (Toronto, 1975) and W. W. Fitzhugh and J. S. Olin, *Archaeology and the Frobisher Voyages* (Washington, 1993); I. Nöel Hume, *The Virginia Adventure. Roanoke to James Towne: An Archaeological and Historical Odyssey* (New York, 1994); S. D. Hurry, M. E. Sullivan, T. B. Riordan, and H. M. Miller, *Once the Metropolis of Maryland': The History and Archaeology of Maryland's First Capital* (St Mary's, Maryland, 2001); compare with H. C. Forman, *Jamestown and St Mary's: Buried Cities of Romance* (Baltimore, 1938).

8 See H. M Colvin, J. Summerson, M. Biddle, J. R. Hale, and M. Merriman, *The History of the King's Works, Vol. IV 1485–1660 (Part II)*, (London, 1982).

9 H. M. Colvin, D. R. Ransome, and J. Summerson, *The History of the King's Works, Vol. IV 1485–1660 (Part I)*, (London, 1975), pp. 373–5.

10 Described by S. G. Ellis, *Tudor Ireland: Crown, Community and Conflict of Cultures 1470–1600* (London and New York, 1985), pp. 256–60, 266–7; refined in his *Tudor Frontiers and Noble Power: The Making of the British State* (Oxford, 1995), which concerns the reign of Henry VIII.

11 See M. MacCarthy-Morrogh, *The Munster Plantation: English Migration to Southern Ireland 1583-1641* (Oxford, 1986), and D. B. Quinn, 'The Munster Plantation: problems and opportunities', *J. Cork Hist. and Archaeol. Soc.* 71 (1966), pp. 19–40. See also Dunlop, 'The plantation of Munster'.

12 R. H. Buchanan, 'Towns and plantations,' in W. Nolan (ed.), *The Shaping of Ireland: The Geographic Perspective* (Dublin, 1986), pp. 85–98. Robinson is quoted on p. 93. R. F. Foster, *Modern Ireland 1600–1972* (New York, 1988), repeats the statement, but asserts that Ulster 'town organization was not as sophisticated as Cork plantation towns like Bandon and Mallow', referring to the second Munster Plantation of the 1600s. Concerning Ulster towns, though, he finds American comparisons 'more relevant than English ones' though 'urban growth was healthier than in contemporary Maryland and Virginia', p. 75. A broader view of the factors that transformed Irish settlement in the sixteenth and seventeenth centuries is provided by W. J. Smyth, 'Ireland a colony: settlement implications of the revolution in military–administrative, urban and ecclesiastical structures, c.1550 to c.1730', in T. Barry (ed.), *A History of Settlement in Ireland* (London and New York, 2000), pp. 158–86.

13 Nicholas Canny argues that the leading families of the Pale pushed for an Irish monarchy to have a government they could dominate. He also points out the similarities between the defences of the Pale and those of Calais: *The Elizabethan Conquest of Ireland: A Pattern Established 1567-76* (New York, 1976), pp. 33–4.

14 D. B. Quinn, 'Ireland and sixteenth century European expansion', *Hist. Studies* I (1958), pp. 20–32.

15 R. Dunlop, 'The plantation of Leix and Offaly', *English Hist. Rev.* 6 (1891), pp. 61–96.

16 E. P. Cheney, 'Some English conditions surrounding the settlement of Virginia', *American Hist. Rev.* 12 (1907), pp. 507–28. Cheney argues that the Munster colony proved a failure, settlers after 1601 being 'almost lost among the surviving native population', p. 516.

17 Summarized by B. Lacy, 'The archaeology of the Ulster Plantation', in M. Ryan (ed), *Illustrated Archaeology*, pp. 201–6. See also J. P. Mallory, and T. E. McNeill, *The Archaeology of Ulster from Colonization to Plantation*, The Institute of Irish Studies, Queen's University (Belfast, 1982), esp. pp. 299–324; and T. W. Moody, *The Londonderrry Plantation* (Belfast, 1937).

18 Nicholas Canny maintains that the 'total failure of the colonists to assimilate the indigenous population ... and ... loss or poor return of money invested' was because the new settlements were nothing like what had been intended, and 'the single most important factor that compelled this change in direction was the inability of organizers to maintain control over those to whom had been entrusted the task of colonization': 'The

permissive frontier; the problem of social control in English settlements in Ireland and Virginia 1550–1650', in K. R. Andrews, N. P. Canny, and P. E. H. Hair (eds), *The Westward Enterprise: English activities in Ireland, the Atlantic, and America 1480–1650* (Detroit, 1979), pp. 17–44, quote from p.17.

19 See E. Klingelhofer, 'The Renaissance fortifications at Dunboy Castle, 1602: a report on the 1989 excavations', *J. Cork Hist. and Archaeol. Soc.*, 97 (1992), pp. 85–96.

20 Camps and forts of the Elizabethan war are illustrated in Sir Thomas Stafford's *Pacata Hibernia*, which though compiled in 1633 (London), probably made use of original maps retained by Stafford and his mentor, Sir George Carew. The role played by the Tudors in Ireland may have been a lengthy one; Stafford is thought to have been Carew's illegitimate son, and Carew himself may have been one of Henry VIII's illegitimate children.

21 See D. B. Quinn and A. M. Quinn (eds), *The New England Voyages 1602–1608*, Hakluyt Society (London, 1983), pp. 231–41. The schematic drawings contain town plans of circular, rectangular, and polygonal design, often with highly concentric interior designs.

22 *Calendar State of Papers, Ireland*, vol. 7, p. 397.

23 Fynes Moryson, *An Itinerary* (London, 1617; repr. Amsterdam, 1971), p. 26.

24 *Cal. S. P. Ireland*, vol. 2, pp. 588–9.

25 A. J. Sheehan, 'The population of the plantation of Munster: Quinn reconsidered', *J. Cork Hist. and Archaeol. Soc.* 87 (1982), pp. 107–17.

26 J. Andrews, 'Plantation Ireland: a review of settlement history', pp. 140–55 in T. Barry (ed.), *History of Settlement*', p. 152.

27 *Cal. S. P. Ireland*, vol. 3, p. 126.

28 National Library of Ireland MS 22,028; see P. D. A. Harvey, 'Estate surveyors and the spread of the scale–map in England 1550–80', *Landscape History* 15 (1993), pp. 37–49.

29 E. Klingelhofer, 'Elizabethan settlements: Mogeely Castle, Curraglass, and Carrigeen, Co. Cork (Part I)', *J. Cork Hist. and Archaeol. Soc.* 104 (1999), pp. 97–11.

30 *Cal. S. P. Ireland* vol. 4, p. 170.

31 Lease for 1615, p. 59 in J. R. Hunter 'Towns in the Ulster Plantation', *Studia Hibernica* 11 (1971), pp. 40–79.

32 I. Nöel Hume and A. Nöel Hume, *The Archaeology of Martin's Hundred* (Philadelphia and Wiliamsburg, 2001), p. 110, Ill. 15, which draws from E. Klingelhofer, 'Excavations at Martins Hundred, Site C (Wolstenholme Towne), 1977–78', 1979 MS report, Department of Archaeology, Colonial Williamsburg Foundation.

33 E. Klingelhofer, 'Elizabethan settlements: Mogeely Castle, Curraglass, and Carrigeen, Co. Cork (Part II), *J. Cork Hist. and Archaeol. Soc.* 105 (2000), pp. 144–74.

34 See A. J. Sheehan, 'The overthrow of the Munster Plantation', *Irish Sword* 15 (1982–83), pp. 11–22.

35 Sheehan, 'Overthrow', p. 17.

36 *Cal. S.P. Ireland* 7, p. 429.

37 See MacCarthy-Morrogh, *Munster Plantation*, pp. 151–5, for the context of Baltimore's development and the competition among major seventeenth-century landowners like Crooke and Coppinger for the seafaring (and pirate) trade.

38 R. Caulfield, *The Council Book of Kinsale* (Surrey, 1879), p. xxxii., discussed in pp. 106–07, H. Barnby, 'The sack of Baltimore', *J. Cork Hist. and Archaeol. Soc.* 74 (1969), pp. 101–29. Crooke is listed as the 'Soveraigne' and has twelve burgesses, similar to the thirteen burgesses that were the minimum for incorporation of Ulster towns.

39 The account of the raid is taken from Barnby, 'Sack of Baltimore'. One detail of Barnby's reconstruction is unconvincing. Rather than row all the way around Coney Island in full view of the castle and both settlements, it seems more likely the raiders landed at the secure inlet directly south of the cove, and crossed the low field there to attack the settlement from the rear.

40 E. J. Priestly, 'An early 17th century map of Baltimore', *J. Cork Hist. and Archaeol. Soc.* 89 (1984), pp. 55–7. Priestly points out that this map, in the Wentworth Collection in the Sheffield City Library, must have come into Strafford's possession before his departure from Ireland in 1640. He considers the Wentworth map a copy of the one sent to Lord Dorchester, and indeed it is likely that Boyle made several copies.

41 See J. Coombes, 'The sack of Baltimore: a forewarning', *J. Cork Hist. and Archaeol. Soc.* 77 (1972), pp. 60–61. The letter-book of the Earl of Cork contains an account of the raid, in which Boyle also reports information from an escaped captive concerning Turkish plans to return. See Barnby, 'Sack of Baltimore', p.124. Boyle would not have been aware that Dudley Carleton, 1st viscount Dorchester, had already died on 15 February 1632.

42 Priestly, 'Map of Baltimore', p. 56. Priestly finds the map to be generally reliable, in spite of several errors, but he is concerned that the depiction of the castle at Baltimore is radically different from what has existed for centuries.

43 It was Priestly's opinion that the castle contained ten houses; some seem to have been built into the slope below the castle. Recent archaeological work within Baltimore castle has found evidence of domestic structures (E. Cotter, personal communication 2009).

44 For details of Bandon, see MacCarthy-Morrogh, *Munster Plantation*, pp. 253–6. Boyle's letter is cited in Dorothea Townshend, *The Life and Letters of the Great Earl of Cork* (London, 1904), p. 44.

4

Vernacular architecture

RIGO: Some part of the building, mee thinketh, is after the Italian maner.
CONO: Some part of it, being ruinous, I built after my fancie, and such as I
found sounde, I thought yenough for me to keepe the repararations.
Barnaby Googe, 1577[1]

Sixteenth-century Ireland does not fit standard English historical periodization. England had by that time abandoned medieval traditions for nation-state building, a new religious creed, and an essentially new nobility. New architectural forms, as well, appeared in both urban and rural locales, and in both wealthy and less affluent households.[2] Ireland was different in many ways from its forward neighbour, and its sixteenth century was one of retarded change, of resistance to both Renaissance and Reformation. The increasing interest of English monarchs in colonizing Ireland and the subsequent plantations of Munster, Ulster, and other regions in the later sixteenth and early seventeenth century give those decades the name 'Plantation Period'. This chapter considers how architectural developments reflect political and social changes in the last generations of Irish autonomy. It analyzes architectural types and techniques associated with the late Elizabethan colonization of Munster, which may be applicable to early modern Ireland in general. The chapter concludes with a study of the tower-house, which was used widely by both Irish aristocracy and English colonial landowners. A key period in Irish history, the reign of Elizabeth began with a medieval, semi-feudal society and ended with a central state authority and displaced populations.

The Privy Council conceived of the Munster Plantation as a solution to the problem of repeated rebellions by disaffected nobles and their clan followers. Courtiers and capitalists received land grants for the purpose of settling numbers of reliable English farmers and craftsmen on the large, but non-contiguous landholdings confiscated from the traitorous Earl of Desmond, his kinsmen, and supporters. The Plantation began in

1586 and was overthrown in 1598 when the Irish of Munster joined the ongoing Nine Years War in Ulster. The Irish defeat at Kinsale in 1601, or the final surrender of Tyrone in 1603, marks the end of the war and the end of Irish independence. For Munster, it marked a new kind of colonization, with little of the planning, rules, and restraints that had characterized the Munster Plantation.

The Plantation had been at best a partial success, its development hampered by a lack of English settlers who were to form a class of tenant farmers required to fence or hedge their fields and erect English-style houses. The landholding gentleman 'servitors', however, adopted the traditional one-year leases or sharecropping agreements with Irish farmers, who had therefore no incentive to invest in the land or its buildings. The planter Edmund Spenser deplored this practice, which maintained the state of incivility among the tenantry, and argued that long-term leases would lead to a beneficial rebuilding of rural Ireland:

> by the hansomnes of his howse, he shall take more Comforte of his life more safe dwellinge and a delight to kepe his saide howse neate and Clenlye which now being (as they Comonlye are) rather Swynesteades then howses, is the Chiefest Cause of his so bestlye manner of life and salvage Condition lyinge and livinge togeather with his beaste in one house in one rome in one bed that is the cleane strawe or rather the foule dunghill.[3]

Maurice Craig noted in 1982 that efforts to find buildings corresponding to the Munster Plantation were without conspicuous success.[4] This issue is addressed here by analysis of the domestic architectural forms associated with the Munster settlements, followed by observations on Elizabethan Irish colonial architecture in the context of recent archaeological findings.

Varieties of domestic forms

There were six domestic forms of vernacular architecture in the Munster Plantation: town houses; tower-houses; plain and fortified manor houses; farm houses; and service buildings.[5]

Town houses

They certainly must have been built during this period, but there is no sharp difference between previous or later urban domestic structures. Large-scale late and post-medieval merchant houses at Kilkenny and Kilmallock suggest an evolving plan, paralleling changes in English townhouses.[6] Late sixteenth- and early seventeenth-century Munster town

Figure 4.1 Late or post-medieval town-houses in Kilmallock, Co. Limerick.

houses undoubtedly remain behind later facades, as smaller-scale houses
at Kilmallock suggest, but Elizabethan settlers in Munster were planted
on the Earl of Desmond's escheated rural lands, and few would have had
urban homes as well (see Figure 4.1). An exception is the large, free-
standing residence 'Myrtle Grove', sited in Youghal close to the medieval
church of St Mary's.[7] Long ascribed to Sir Walter Raleigh, this building
has multiple gables, clustered chimneys, a front of ashlar masonry and
hood moldings for doors and for rectangular, multiple-light windows
(see Figure 4.2).

Tower-houses

Ubiquitous in Munster, tower-houses were part of a generic group of
fortified aristocratic residences that included the Scottish 'bastle' and the
Border 'peel tower'. Most date to the fifteenth and early sixteenth centuries, and some were built as late as the seventeenth century, but none
has been ascribed to the Plantation per se.[8] Tower-houses with strong

Figure 4.2 View of Myrtle Grove, Youghal, Co. Cork, with St Mary's Church in the foreground, 1842.

Elizabethan associations, though of medieval origin, are Blarney Castle, famous for the Queen's remark about its lord; Barryscourt, burned by its owner rather than permit the English to occupy it; and Kilcolman Castle, where Edmund Spenser composed *The Faerie Queene* (see Figure 5.3). Because plantation grants of manors confiscated from the Desmond lordship often coincided with castelancies, it was easy for English land-

owners to reuse the tower-houses on their properties. Some new elements
of decoration appear in the second half of the sixteenth century, such as
chamfered window jambs and a band of pecked decoration bordering
windows and doors, but the broad dating of this work and of the tower-
houses themselves do not define English occupation.

Manor houses

These decorative features also appear on manor houses. Comprising the
most studied but problematic form of post-medieval architecture, such
buildings should have had the greatest amount of English influence, but
at this time, English manorial architecture was evolving in complex ways
towards the seventeenth- and eighteenth-century country house.[9] A
Munster colonial planter might choose to build a manor house de novo
or to add elements of one to a pre-existing structure, which was the case
at two seignorial seats of Raleigh associates: Spenser's Kilcolman Castle
and Thomas Harriot's Molana Abbey.[10]

Elizabethan manor houses were often laid out in the well-known
'H-plan'. A central hall house was flanked by domestic and service wings,
usually of equal height and similar facade. At the same time, in less pacified Scotland there appeared the 'Z-plan', in which flankers were built at
opposite corners of a structure of several storeys, usually a tower-house.
In addition to these two sixteenth-century architectural types in Britain,
one undefended, the other defended, other plans appeared in Ireland,
with important early examples in Munster. Forms of the fortified house,
its military function recognized by contemporaries as a 'castle', offered
a more spacious alternative to the dark and cramped tower-house.[11]
Indeed, the continued use and even construction of tower-houses into
the 1640s was supplemented by these fortified houses. Built from *ca.*1560
to *ca.*1650, they typically had a symmetrical layout, large multi-light
windows, and a multi-gable roof line, resulting in a better ordered use of
space, more light and air, and more rooms in the topmost floor for children, servants, and storage. David Waterman identified the appearance
of this building type in the late sixteenth century as the first expression in
Ireland of the Renaissance-influenced English architecture, a movement
which would eventually end the construction of traditional buildings.[12]

Further study makes it possible to recognize distinct plan-types among
'castle-houses', and to consider their presence in the Munster plantation.
Retaining the alphabetic nomenclature used by scholars of Elizabethan
architecture, the first type is the 'X-plan', a rectangular multi-storey
structure with a flanker at each corner. The flankers are usually square,

Figure 4.3 Kanturk Castle, Co. Cork.

but occasionally have a trapezoidal 'spear shape', imitating Renaissance bastions of Italian design.[13] Noteworthy Elizabethan X-plan buildings are Archbishop Loftus's Rathfarnham Castle near Dublin (probably 1590s), the McCarthy seat of Kanturk Castle, Co. Cork (*ca.* 1600), and the brick-built Mountjoy Castle in Ulster, completed in 1605, the small scale of which fits its military and administrative functions (see Figures 4.3, 2.11). As Craig noted, fortified houses were commonly built by men in senior leadership positions.[14] These early examples all appear in areas of English military activity – the Pale, the Munster Plantation, and the occupied portion of Ulster.

Another 'colonial' type of fortified dwelling or castle-house was a reduced version of the X-plan, though it cannot be determined if this form actually began later. Here, flankers were built at the corners of the

Figure 4.4 Rear view of Mallow Castle, Co. Cork.

building's front wall only. Two other flankers often appear at the far end of a walled 'bawn' enclosure. The layout of the residence suggests an inverted 'Y', because a tower or projection centrally positioned on the building's rear wall offered close defence to the otherwise unprotected face, as well as stair access. The earliest example of a Y-plan house is

Figure 4.5 Sherborne Castle, Dorset. The upper storey and wings are seventeenth-century additions.

Mallow Castle, rebuilt by Sir Thomas Norris, the President of Munster, after its destruction in 1598[15] (see Figures 1.7, 4.4). Mallow Castle is three storeys high and has polygonal flankers, a not uncommon shape on late medieval castles and fortifications, but perhaps first used in the Elizabethan Renaissance by Raleigh at Sherborne Castle (Lodge) in Dorset (see Figure 4.5). It is likely that the Y-plan further devolved into both the simpler T-plan house without flankers and the U-plan with flankers but without a stair tower, both of which are found at bawn 'castles' of the seventeenth-century Ulster Plantation.[16]

Farm houses

By far the most common residence of English colonists, farm houses made up perhaps ten or twenty times the number of manor houses and castles, according to how many families each grantee managed to plant in Munster. No surviving farm house in Munster has yet been ascribed to the Plantation, and indeed it is unlikely that many survived the destruction of English properties in the 1598 uprising, when all but a handful of strongholds outside the walled cities were lost by the English. But while Elizabethan farm houses are no longer present, they were shown on contemporary maps as standing among fields or in villages (see Figure 3.7). Raleigh's map of the Mogeely estate depicts English-style houses, probably timber-framed and one-and-a-half or two storeys high, with a central chimney and framed doors and windows, distinguishing them

Figure 4.6 Cob-walled cabins at Bandon, Co. Cork.

clearly from the native Irish oval-shaped, dome-roofed dwellings without
window or chimney[17] (see Figure 1.9). At some point, and it may be earlier
than documented, a native tradition of one-storey structures with 'cob' or
clay walls, but with central doorways and flanking windows, becomes the
typical cottages or cabins of modern history, often row-built, with small
gardens behind (see Figure 4.6).

Service buildings

These utilitarian structures must have been built in their hundreds,
but none so far has been firmly identified as belonging to the Munster
Plantation, nor do contemporary drawings depict numbers sufficient
for comment. It seems probable that English settlers used materials
and models most familiar to them, like the large estate barn that served
Mogeely Castle manor (see Figure 4.7).

Colonial buildings

Archaeological research offers an important new source of information
about Elizabethan Ireland, and especially about its architecture. Excavations have been able to amend Maurice Craig's comment about the failure

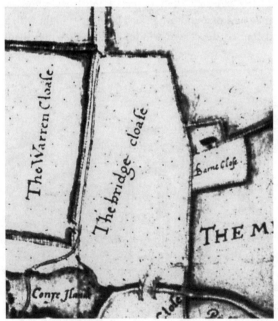

Figure 4.7 Detail
of barn in Mogeely
Estate Map.

to find Munster Plantation buildings, and four observations about English colonial buildings in Munster are presented here.

First, the continuity of residence between Irish and colonial settlements was limited and does not appear to have been a determining factor of colonization. Certainly some sites were occupied by the English after evicting native inhabitants. We have seen that the Mogeely Castle estate map suggests such was the case at the Carrigeen hamlet there, which has been supported by archaeological excavation.[18] On the other hand, the number of 'Newtown' place-names in Munster no doubt indicate sites without continuity of settlement. Colonized places like Tallow, Curraglass, and later Clonakilty and Bandon were also essentially new starts, regardless of what previous site histories may have been. As noted in Chapter 3, planned towns and villages were part of a fully developed settlement pattern for Munster, at least on paper. Native Irish *clachan* hamlets and pre-existing Anglo-Irish cities and port towns remained, but the great change for Munster lay in the integrated, enclosed, field systems and in the commercial and industrial centres such as Tallow on the Cork–Waterford border, where iron works and timber yards sent commodities down the river Bride to the Blackwater harbour at Youghal.

Second, few forms of vernacular architecture seem to have been taken from existing Irish structures. Tower-houses were certainly adopted as seignorial seats, but the manor houses and farm houses in which the majority of settlers lived cannot claim to have derived from an Irish architectural tradition.

Third, an Irish 'colonial' style of vernacular architecture, as distinctive as the seventeenth-century 'Plantation Gothic' religious architecture found in Ulster, Munster, and Virginia, appeared in certain forms of manor house.[19] These were the X-plan and the Y-plan. Some of these buildings also had decorative elements found in late Munster tower-houses: chamfering and decorative bands around windows and doors.

Fourth, archaeology in the past decades has recovered data on sites associated with the Munster Plantation. Identified on the Mogeely estate map, the excavated site of an English-style timber-frame farmhouse was found to comprise a rectangular footing of limestone rubble in a heavy lime mortar, set into a 'leveling up' deposit of mixed clay and gravel.[20] Other sites in Munster, moreover, reveal that the colonists used clay instead of mortar to bond low stone walls for timber-framed buildings and perhaps in even higher stone walls. This bonding has been found in farmers' houses at the Carrigeen hamlet on the Mogeely estate, in several structures at Kilcolman Castle, in early seventeenth-century buildings inside the Roche family seat of Glanworth Castle, and in a late seven-teenth-century house near Limerick.[21] A possible reason for the use of these non-traditional kinds of masonry bonding is lack of time, or more likely, lack of expertise in the preparation of mortar, which was consid-ered a skilled craft.[22] Additional architectural details have come from the excavation of Edmund Spenser's house at Kilcolman Castle, which is discussed more fully in Chapter 5. The fragments of diamond-shaped panes of casement window glass, and the evidence of white plastered walls and evenly spaced floorboards confirm that his 'fair stone house' was a building of some refinement.[23]

Statements about the vernacular architecture of the Munster Plantation lead to parallels and contrasts. There is painfully little surviving archi-tecture, and archaeology has much to undertake here, but detailed maps and surveys of other Tudor colonial areas can provide a broader context of post-medieval colonization in Ireland.[24] The remarkably detailed *ca.* 1560 picture-map of Carrickfergus, Co. Antrim (see Figure 2.14) portrays the walled town as having only three types of domestic buildings: twelve tower-houses, many one-storey-and-a-loft row houses lying parallel to the street, and scores of randomly placed, windowless, dome-shaped Irish cabins.[25] The 1560s English quasi-urban settlements of Philipstown and Maryborough in King's and Queen's counties, respectively, are shown by maps (see Figure 3.3). and field inspection to have comprised a square fort (with or without bastions) joined to a rectangular, walled town, with regu-larly arranged houses of one-and-a-half storeys with central chimneys.[26] Contemporary Elizabethan ventures, like the plantations attempted in Ulster by Sir Thomas Smith and the Earl of Essex, and the one near Cork by St Leger and Grenville, proved either too small, too poorly organized, or too short-lived to provide architectural information.[27]

In Ulster and Wexford, however, valuable architectural studies of early seventeenth-century English settlements have been undertaken.[28] These Jacobean plantations, like the earlier Munster colony, display a concern for order and defence. Rolf Loeber's field studies investigating Sir Thomas Rotheram's 1621 survey of the north Wexford settlements showed that the typical planter built 'a main house with one or two flankers adjoining a walled court or bawn, about twelve to thirteen feet [*c.* 4m] high, which was reinforced by one or two flankers'.[29] Plantation villages of farmers' and artisans' houses have not survived there; nor have unsurveyed tenant buildings of timber or sod, the lowest level of housing. In studies by Philip Robinson and Brooke Blades, most Ulster villages in Thomas Raven's 1622 maps conformed to what was on the ground: ordered rows

Figure 4.8 Molana Abbey, Co. Waterford, residence of Raleigh's scientist, Thomas Harriot.

of timber-framed houses with central chimney stacks, adjacent to a forti-fied stone manor house with a wall-and-flanker bawn.[30] This was clearly an improvement on conditions in Elizabethan Munster, where evidence for nucleated rural settlement shows no accompanying fortification, and where defensible manor houses and castles stood among scattered settle-ments.[31] The examples of Myrtle Grove and Molana Abbey (see Figures 4.1, 4.8). show that undefended manor houses were not only built (or rebuilt), but preferred, yet others did have some element of fortification. One is reminded that the collapse of the Munster Plantation was not, after all, because the 'signorial' seats of the colony were unfortified, but because outside the cities, what defences Munster had, were insufficiently maintained and manned.

Tower-houses and castle-houses

A key element, perhaps *the* key element, to understanding Ireland in these centuries between 1400 and 1600 is the residential castle, in some documents called 'fortalice,' but by modern scholars commonly identi-fied as the 'tower-house,' a structure that appears across late medieval Western Europe.[32] There are hundreds of ruined tower-houses in Ireland today, and several dozen that are complete or nearly so (see Figure 4.9).

This type of castle contained two main elements, a residential tower perhaps 10m square and 15m high, and a defended courtyard perhaps 40m square, called a 'bailey' by the English and a 'bawn' by the Irish. The tower's base usually had a strong batter, and the roof line was crenellated. The single entrance was defended above by a projecting machicolation,

Figure 4.9 Conna Castle, Co. Cork, a typical Irish tower-house.

and a 'murder hole' was often placed in the ceiling over the entrance lobby. There were at least four floors, the lowest being a vaulted cellar, above which lay public and service rooms, and at the top, bedrooms for the castelain's family. The bawn wall was perhaps 4m high, and built against it was the great hall for business, judgment, and entertainment, and outbuildings like the kitchen, granary, and stables.

The tower-house was the last castle in Europe, but it has only recently attracted the depth of study that has been directed to early castle forms of motte-and-bailey and ringwork, or tracing castle development in stone through Anjevin keeps, Plantagenet mural towers, and Staufer geometrical designs. By the early sixteenth century, technology and politics changed the role of castles. Gunpowder permitted cannon and effective siegecraft. The modern state possessed the resources and the resolve to eradicate private armies and their castles. Pioneers of military architectural studies, like Sir Charles Oman, argued that the siege train made castles irrelevant to the final outcome of a conflict. Warfare was henceforth determined by efficiency of mobilization: the largest force and the fastest movement. By 1500, Oman claimed that 'even a show of defensive strength was abandoned' at English aristocratic residences, and Henry VIII's coastal artillery 'castles' were misnamed forts.[33] In the 1950s, Sidney Toy viewed the tower-house as a stage of transition from castle to mansion, beginning in the late fourteenth century with the appearance of a residential tower in a rectangular, moated castle (Bodiam, Ferrarra, Mantua). The tower was then detached from the inner bailey to be independently defensible (Vincennes, Warkworth). In the later fifteenth century, the English residential tower or keep became increasingly impressive and stylish (Tattershall, Ashby de la Zouche) (see Figure 6.1), while in the Border counties of England and Scotland, smaller 'peel towers' sheltered dependents and their herds from sixteenth-century cross-border raiding.[34]

Sidney Toy identified the origin of the English tower-house as deriving from the residential tower within a larger castle, so the Scottish or Border peel tower would be a late flourishing of that type. It would be logical to assume that the Irish tower-house had the same derivation. Recently, however, David Newman Johnson has argued for greater continuity between the Norman donjon and the tower-house, observing that the early examples of the tower-house were in an international style, and only the later ones exhibit characteristic Irish features.[35] Another scholar, Conrad Cairns, has traced the erection of government-sponsored 'fortalice' tower-houses to the early 1300s, which undercuts Toy's argument, as the Irish examples preceded the independent defence of domestic quarters in large English and French castles.[36] The reverse influence, from Ireland to England and France, is not credible, and the likeliest case at present is for a separate origin of the Irish tower-house. As for its demise, the argument that cannon doomed the tower has been deflated by Tom McNeill's observation that 'the move away from anything we can really call a castle, and toward country houses, had started well before the middle of the [sixteenth] century.'[37] Whatever may be their architectural ancestry, the early fortalices would have best served as compact structures for small garrisons. As the late medieval state was increasingly incapable of exercising its authority, the lesser nobility may well have usurped fortalices to control the countryside, and later accumulated the resources needed to build other or larger tower-houses to accommodate their needs.

As the centre of a medieval manor and the stronghold for a clan's landholdings, the tower-house would normally defend a family, its dependants, and their possessions. Increasing numbers of tower-houses over time imply a weakening of English authority and respect for royal law. Terry Barry saw the spread of tower-houses and fortified friaries in the fifteenth century testifying to both the availability of resources for such construction and the shift away from central authority to regional power bases.[38] For Barry, the fact that tower-houses were constructed in both rural and urban settings indicates how thoroughly Ireland underwent the change (see Figure 4.10). Their appearances in urban churchyards and rural monasteries, however, show more than a shift in authority from central to regional. A serious breakdown in government control seems to have led to the erection of ecclesiastical tower-houses as an alternative to new protective roles for lay patrons.

The characteristics and history of the tower-house, rather than its origins, were analyzed in Harold Leask's seminal work, *Irish Castles*.[39] He presented an evolution by which the simple, single-chamber tower of rectangular or round plan was progressively enlarged and developed internal divisions and corner stair or garderobe (privy) towers. Some of the late tower-houses would double in size (Blarney) and have four flanking corner towers (Barryscourt), the front pair of which would sometimes be arched over (Bunratty).

Later on, in the Plantation Period, these 'supertowers' were rivaled in status and comfort by new, towered and gabled structures, 'castle-houses' (Kanturk, Coppinger's Court).[40] Constructed in late Elizabethan and early Stuart times, the castle-house usually stood alone (Mallow, Rathfarnham), but was sometimes added to an existing tower-house. We have seen that the common Elizabethan manor house cross-wing H plan and

Figure 4.10 Tynte's Castle, an urban tower-house in Youghal, Co. Cork.

half-court E and U plans, and the add-on T plan, were joined by castle-house types with recognizable X, Y, and Z plans.[41] Coinciding with Elizabethan colonization and spurred – if not initiated – by it, the castle-house had essentially replaced the tower-house before construction of both ceased by the middle of the seventeenth century with the spreading civil wars and Cromwell's regime. Tadhg O'Keeffe observed a 'radical change' that ended castle construction *ca*.1600 and simultaneously 'bifurcated' architectural evolution into houses with a level of comfort as well as musket defences and Renaissance-style artillery forts with garrisons but no domestic component[42] (see Figures 1.6, 6.8).

Beginning in 1611, a generation after the change began toward castle-house construction, Ulster Plantation castles were erected to defend the

Anglo-Scottish settlements that replaced evicted native communities.[43]
The Plantation castle there could be a tower-house or a castle-house,
even an undefended manor house. But it was set in a high-walled bawn,
usually with two towers or flankers set on opposite corners. Building
details sometimes show a Scottish influence, and in general these bawn
castles were built along stronger military lines than their counterparts in
the south, perhaps reflecting the English army service shared by many of
the new landowners.

The developing manor house is an essential element of late medieval England, but where did the lesser Irish nobility live before they
had tower-houses? Many tower-houses exhibit evidence for adjacent or
attached halls. It is possible that a bawn-and-hall arrangement preceded
the tower- house. As we have seen, tower-houses seem to have appeared
first in government schemes for regional defence, but with increasingly chaotic conditions, they were adopted by the nobility for domestic
protection. The large numbers of tower-houses may represent the failure
of English government to make headway against Celtic institutions, but
they do not necessarily support an argument based on ethnicity. It is not
that Ireland had so many residential castles of the lesser nobility, but that
England had notably fewer such castles than the rest of Europe. Conrad
Cairns was correct to point out that the frequency of similar structures
in Spain, France, and Germany resembles Ireland more than England.[44]

It was not the Irish, but the English who were outside the mainstream
of late medieval developments. This behaviour by the English aristocracy
is unlikely to have been caused by their participation in Parliamentary
decision-making, or by the new wealth and opportunities that the professional and merchant upper bourgeoisie offered them through marriage.
Broad judicial corruption revealed in the Paston family letters and the
ease of treason during the late fifteenth-century twenty-year series of
dynastic and military struggles known as the Wars of the Roses, testify
to an English nobility with no more civic sensibility than the Germans or
French. The claim that the English lesser aristocracy was unable to accu-
mulate the resources needed to build even minor castles is questioned by
their construction of new manor houses. The real difference, especially
for the first century of tower-houses, was that no sustained wars were
fought within England. Because the battles of the Hundred Years War
took place in France, England enjoyed domestic peace and what order
strong kings provided. And with no tradition of private wars, English
royal authority was maintained at a higher level than elsewhere, until the
Wars of the Roses. In other countries, for centuries this had been and

would be the normal condition; hence their continued need for defended residences. The absence of what today would be called 'security forces' on the Scottish–English border similarly led to the construction of peel towers there.

In Michael Thompson's examination of late medieval castle developments, the tower-house as a type of castle is largely restricted to Ireland, Lowland Scotland, and the Border counties. Thompson proposed that the courtyard manor house common to the rest of England was important to a society for which sizeable retinues still earned status, but became increasingly expensive to maintain. For various castle types, small size or elaborate defences infer limited garrisons in societies where large retinues were rare, or only mobilized for field combat. The few late medieval castles built on English soil were erected by men who had won fortunes in the Hundred Years War and wanted their new homes to reflect their achievement. Thompson suggests an evolutionary connection between the twin gate towers of the thirteenth century, the single, large gate tower of the fourteenth century, and the great residential tower of England along with its small-scale version, the Irish tower-house, of the fifteenth century.[45] The heavier English armaments ensured that in England, tower-houses would be 'show-castles' for the display of status, while a lower level of available weaponry in Ireland gave substance to a tower-house defence, at least until 1600.[46]

Colonial construction

Archaeological work of the past two decades has added new information about the construction and layout of Irish tower-houses. This research has just begun, and much of the information is unpublished.[47] Yet one pattern has already appeared. As we have seen, the sixteenth-century lords enlarged existing tower-houses and erected more complex examples. In the Plantation Period, new English owners reused tower-houses, but made little change to the defences of both tower and bawn. New or replacement structures were normally built into the bawn wall, yet in many cases their masonry was not bonded with mortar, but with clay. This change marks an obvious break in the architectural tradition of Irish castle building, one that may well reveal the tastes or limitations of the new settlers. Several explanations come to mind. The builders may have had limited resources and lacked money, experienced workers, or time to erect more spacious and useful accommodations in what was most likely a competition for status. Simultaneous construction work at scores of sites, under a deadline mandated by the royal grant of land, could have led to hasty building techniques. Clay bonding was not new to Ireland, but it seems not to have been used in major structures in castles before. The ubiquity of limestone would rule out a lack of materials, though workers skilled in lime burning and mortar mixing could have been in short supply. Alternatively, the builders may have employed less substantial bonding techniques because the wall load was lighter. A change to timber-framed buildings, seated on stone foundations at knee or waist height would explain the clay bonding. In any case, the new owners took less care in their considerations for defence, in both construction techniques and in the lack of updated military features, perhaps because they themselves lacked a recent tradition of self-defence, or because they assumed it was no longer necessary.

England under the Tudors saw the residences of the educated classes acquire legal protections equal to the defences formerly provided by castles. This was not the case in Ireland, where the last castles in Western Europe still safeguarded family and fortune, but such protections may have seemed no longer necessary when English planters replaced feuding Irish nobles. Although tower-houses continued to dominate the local inhabitants and give the new owners the status of a feudal aristocracy, the O'Neill uprising of 1598 sacked all but four English houses and castles

Coppinger's Court. (some windows restored).

Figure 4.11 Coppinger's Court, drawn by Harold Leask.

outside the walled cities of Munster. Not only the English, but now the Irish as well, had proved the tower-house obsolete. In the following generation, it would cease to be the standard residence of the landowning class.

Tudor policy in Ireland had long promoted a 'cultural imperialism' that continued well beyond the sixteenth century, the only variable being the means to that end: 'Anglicization *versus* colonization.'[48] Architectural changes in Munster stemmed from a spreading European Renaissance classicism as well as a weakening of the functional, vernacular tradition. English colonists brought along their own vernacular traditions, but the sudden demand for housing in the late 1580s and the subsequent scarcity of skilled builders apparently led to the lower standard of construction techniques now demonstrated archaeologically. As the agricultural landscape of Ireland was dramatically – and permanently – changed by the imposition of English enclosed fields, so too the houses of the men who owned and worked the land were no longer the same. For the commoners, the rectangular English stone or half-timbered house pushed the rounded Irish cabin into the hills and woods as a less civilized form of habitation.

While judiciously adopting the tower-houses of the old society, English gentry of the Tudor-Stuart 'Ascendency' also raised structures appropriate to their new status. Mansions and manor houses were usually chosen, and perhaps preferred, as seats of estates. In Munster and later plantations, castle-houses retained an element of fortification – bawns, flankers, gun loops, and crenelation – sensible precautions, but perhaps also revealing that repeated declarations of Irish savagery failed in some way to convince the settlers of their own superiority, and failed also to validate their undeniable claim to the land. It is a measure of the power of Tudor-Stuart cultural imperialism, though, that some of the greatest examples of these semi-fortified mansions, the Earl of Ormond's house at Carrick-on-Suir, the McCarthys' Kanturk Castle, and the later Coppinger's Court (see Figure 4.11), were built not for planters, but for leading Anglicized and Anglo-Irish families who sought to maintain their independent status and influence by adopting the symbols and structures of the new society.

Notes

1 Barnaby Googe, *Foure Bookes of Husbandry, collected by M. Conradus Heresbachus ... Newely Englished, and increased, by Barnabe Googe, Esquire* (London, 1577; repr. Amsterdam, 1971), p. 9. Googe was a Cambridge graduate and cousin of Cecil. In 1574 he began his service in Ireland, where he may have translated and expanded this work, which he dedicated to Sir William Fitzwilliam, the former Lord Deputy. Provost Marshal of Connaught from 1582, he died in 1594; see E. M. Hinton, *Ireland Through Tudor Eyes* (Philadephia, 1935), p. 32.

2 A brief summary of social change and new building is found in P. Williams, *Life in Tudor England* (New York, 1964). For broad reviews of English architectural developments, see M. W. Barley, 'Rural housing in England', in J. Thirsk (ed.), *The Agrarian History of England and Wales Vol. IV 1500-1640* (Cambridge, 1967), pp. 696–766; and C. Platt, *The Great Buildings of Tudor and Stuart England* (London, 1994).

3 Edmund Spenser, 'View of the state of Ireland', in R. Gottfried, *Spenser's Prose Works* (Baltimore, 1949), pp. 41–231, quote from p. 135 (ll. 2573–9). But see the debate on Spenser's attitudes and intentions concerning Irish 'incivility', as presented by Nicholas Canny, Ciaran Brady, Patricia Coughlan, and Anne Fogarty, in P. Coughlan (ed.), *Spenser in Ireland: An Interdisciplinary Perspective* (Cork, 1989).

4 Maurice Craig, *The Architecture of Ireland from the earliest times to 1880* (London and Dublin, 1982), p. 123. See also C. O'Danachair, *Ireland's Vernacular Architecture* (Cork, 1975).

5 R. W. Brunskill, *Illustrated Handbook of Vernacular Architecture* (London, 1971), pp. 22–4, divides domestic residences into size types: Great House, Large House, Small House, and Cottage. The first two types may merge into our manor house, the third is our farm house, and the fourth would be Irish-constructed.

6 See J. Schofield, *Medieval London Houses* (London and New Haven, 1995), especially pp. 61-93; and D. Crossley, *Post-Medieval Archaeology in Britain* (Leicester and New York, 1990), pp. 75–97.

7 Limited observations of the above-ground fabric of Myrtle Grove suggest that Raleigh radically adapted a section of the St Mary's college residence, perhaps even reversing the face of the building. My thanks to Mr and Mrs Murray for their hospitality.

8 See H. Leask, *Irish Castles and Castellated Houses* (Dundalk, 1986; first edn 1941). See also J. N. Healy, *The Castles of County Cork* (Cork, 1988).

9 The evolution of the manor houses is extensively discussed in M. W. Barley, 'Rural housing in England', pp. 696–766; C. Platt, *The Great Rebuildings of Tudor and Stuart England. Revolutions in Architectural Taste* (London, 1994); and M. W. Thompson, *The Decline of the Castle* (Cambridge, 1987).

10 The better-studied Ulster plantation has several examples of such reuse. See P. Mallory and T. E. McNeill, *The Archaeology of Ulster from Colonization to Plantation* (Belfast, 1982), pp. 309-10. The example of Kilcolman is based on excavation, and that of Molana on personal inspection of the site.

11 Examples and commentary, though not the terms 'X plan' and 'Z plan', will be found in Craig, *Architecture of Ireland* , pp. 111–35; and P. Kerrigan, *Castles and Fortifications in Ireland 1485-1945* (Cork, 1995), pp. 64–72. N. McCullen and V. Mulvin, *A Lost Tradition. The Nature of Architecture in Ireland* (Dublin, 1987), pp. 44–55, covers much of the same material, but only in terms of plan and function, without clear chronological and geographic distinctions.

12 D. M. Waterman, 'Some Irish seventeenth-century houses and their architectural ancestry', in M. Jope (ed.), *Studies in Building History. Essays dedicated to B. H. St J. O'Neil* (London, 1961), pp. 251–74, ref. p. 252. Emphasizing their geographic propensity, Waterman labelled them 'Munster houses'.

13 Examples of round flankers appear later in Northern Ireland; see Kerrigan, *Castles and Fortifications*, p. 70, Fig. 41.

14 Craig, *Architecture of Ireland*, p. 118.

15 The present structure of Mallow Castle may not be that in which Norris lived before the Nine Years War. Without detailed architectural study, it is safer to assume that its rebuilding was probably started by Norris and completed after his death in 1599 by his daughter Elizabeth and son-in law Sir John Jephson. Both Thomas and his brother, Sir John Norris, died at Mallow Castle, the latter according to local legends, after an encounter with the Devil. See J. S. Nolan, *Sir John Norreys and the Elizabethan Military World* (Exeter, 1997), p. 238; H. G. Leask, 'Mallow Castle, Co. Cork', *J. Cork Hist. and Archaeol. Soc.* 49 (1944), pp. 19–24; and H. F. Berry, 'The English settlement in Mallow under the Jephson family', *J. Cork Hist. and Archaeol. Soc.* 12 (1906), pp. 1–26.

16 For Ulster T-plan houses, see Kerrigan, *Castles and Fortification*, pp. 70–1.

17 Mogeely estate map, National Library of Ireland MS 22,028.

18 See E. Klingelhofer, 'Proto-colonial archaeology: the case of Elizabethan Ireland', in P. Funari, M. Hall, and S. Jones (eds), *Back from the Edge: Archaeology in History* (London, 1999), pp. 64–79.

19 Examples are the Londonderry and Lisburn cathedrals, Ulster; St Luke's, Smithfield, Virginia; and Christ Church, Bandon, Co. Cork. For a general discussion, see McCullough and Mulvin, *Lost Tradition* , pp. 75–7; for Ulster plantation churches, see Mallory and McNeill, *Archaeology of Ulster*, pp. 313–14.

20 E. Klingelhofer, 'Elizabethan settlement: Mogeely Castle, Curraglass, and Carrigeen, Co. Cork (Part I)', *J. Cork Hist. and Archaeol. Soc.* 104 (1999), pp. 97–110, and Part II, 105 (2000), pp. 155–74.

21 Discussed in E. Klingelhofer, 'Edmund Spenser at Kilcolman Castle: the archaeological evidence', *Post-Medieval Archaeol.* 39 (2005), pp. 133–54. See also C. Manning, 'A Sheila-na-Gig from Glanworth Castle, Co. Cork, pp. 278–82, in E. Rynne and H. M. Roe (eds), *Figures from the Past* (Dun Loaghaire, 1987), and *Clough Outer: A Midlands Castle in Co. Cavan* (Bray, 1999); and M. Ponsford, 'Post-medieval Britain and Ireland in 1990', in *Medieval Archaeol.* 25 (1991), pp. 115–70, ref. pp. 142–3.

22 See L.F. Salzman, *Building in England down to 1546: A Documentary History* (Oxford, 1952), pp. 149–54. The burning of lime was considered skilled work, though the actual mixing of the lime and sand to produce mortar was by 'mortarmen' who were unskilled labourers.

23 Klingelhofer, 'Kilcolman Castle', pp. 145, 149.

24 A concise review is given by R. H. Buchanon in 'Towns and plantations, 1500-1700', in W. Nolan (ed.), *The Shaping of Ireland. The Geographic Perspective* (Cork and Dublin, 1986), pp. 84–98. A more detailed account is by R. Loeber in *The Geography and Practice of English Colonization in Ireland from 1534 to 1609*, Irish Settlement Series 3 (Athlone, 1991). Important details in the maps by Barthelet, cartographer to Lord Mountjoy, appear in C. O'Danachair, 'Representations of houses on some Irish maps of c.1600', in G. Jenkins (ed.), *Studies in Folk Life. Essays in Honour of Iowert C. Peate*, (London, 1969), pp. 91–103.

25 British Library, Cotton MS Augustus I. ii. 42. Reproduced in Harvey, *Maps in Tudor England* (Chicago and London, 1993a) p. 99. A few of the houses have chimneys (perhaps drawn later). Only one seems to be at a gable, the others are placed centrally.

26 Kerrigan, *Castles and Fortifications*, pp. 29–32.

27 These activities are well covered in Nicholas P. Canny, *The Elizabethan Conquest of Ireland: A Pattern Established 1565-76* (New York, 1977), pp. 77–92.

28 In Ulster, Mallory and McNeill distinguish between the houses of the gentry and those of a vernacular tradition: *Archaeology of Ulster*, pp. 311–14. For Wexford, see R. Loeber and M. Stouthamer-Loeber, 'The lost architecture of the Wexford Plantation', in K. Whelan (ed.), *Wexford: History and Society. Interdisciplinary Essays on the History of an Irish County* (Dublin, 1987), pp. 173–200.

29 Loeber and Stouthamer-Loeber, 'Wexford Plantation', p.182. The Loebers further note

that sixteenth-century Wexford saw the transition from tower-houses to the 'hall type tower houses', at least on the south coast of the county, p. 184.

30 B. S. Blades, 'English villages in the Londonderry Plantation', *Post-Medieval Archaeol.* 20 (1986), pp. 257–69, and '"In the manner of England": tenant housing in the Londonderry Plantation', *Ulster Folklife* 27 (1981), pp. 39–56; P. Robinson, 'Vernacular housing in Ulster in the seventeenth century', *Ulster Folklife* 25 (1979), pp. 1–28, and '"English" houses built at Moneymore, County Londonderry, *c.* 1615', *Post-Medieval Archaeol.* 17 (1983), pp. 47–64.

31 See M. Salter, *Castles and Stronghouses of Ireland* (Malvern, 1993), for a concise introduction to the topic and a well-chosen gazetteer.

32 For a brief introduction to the topic, see M. W. Thompson, *The Decline of the Castle* (Cambridge, 1987), pp. 22–6.

33 C. Oman, *Castles* (London, 1926; repr. New York, 1978), pp. 22, 23.

34 S. Toy, *A History of Fortification* (London, 1955), pp. 212–29. See also J. Zeune, 'Perfecting the tower house: post-medieval Scottish castellated architecture', *Fortress* 10 (1991), pp. 24–30; 11 (1991), pp. 14–28.

35 D. N. Johnson, 'Later medieval castles' pp. 188–92 in M. Ryan, (ed.), *The Illustrated Archaeology of Ireland* (Dublin, 1992).

36 C. Cairns, 'The Irish tower house – a military view', *Fortress* 11 (1991) pp. 3–13. His findings would put the tower-house over a century before the 'ten pound' castles that Henry VI subsidized in 1429 to defend the Pale.

37 T. McNeill, *Castles in Ireland: Feudal Power in a Gaelic World* (London and New York, 1997), p. 228. He concludes the argument: 'Artillery which did not become effective before the 1650s cannot have caused a change visible before 1600'.

38 T. B. Barry, *The Archaeology of Medieval Ireland*, (London and New York, 1987), p. 181. But for a different perspective, see also T. O'Keeffe, 'Castle-building and the construction of identity: contesting narratives about medieval Ireland', *Irish Geography* 33 (2000), pp. 69–88.

39 See Leask, *Irish Castles*. For comparative plans, see McCullen and Mulvin, *A Lost Tradition*, pp. 37, 38.

40 Here I have modified Leask's term 'castellated house' to 'castle-house', as more convenient and reflecting a typological relationship to the tower-house. See also D. M. Waterman, 'Some Irish seventeenth-century houses'.

41 Eric Klingelhofer, 'Vernacular architecture of the Munster Plantation', paper presented to the American Historical Association, Atlanta, 1996. For comparative plans, see McCullen and Mulvin, *Lost Tradition*, pp. 46, 47.

42 T. O'Keeffe, 'Barryscourt Castle and the Irish Tower-House', in J. Ludlow and N. Jameson (eds), *Medieval Ireland: The Barryscourt Lectures I–X* (Kinsale, 2004), pp. 1–32.

43 An overview of Ulster Plantation bawn castles is given in Kerrigan, *Castles and Fortifications*, pp. 68–80.

44 Cairns, 'Irish tower house', p. 3.

45 Thompson, *The Decline of the Castle*, pp. 71–102.

46 For a seminal study on the transition from castle to mansion, see P. Dixon and B. Lot, 'The courtyard and the tower: contexts and symbols in the development of late medieval great houses', *J. British Archaeol. Assoc.* 146 (1993), pp. 93-101; for an airing of scholars' views on interpreting roles played by castles, see M. Johnson, *Behind the Castle Gate: From Medieval to Renaissance* (London and New York, 2002), pp. 106–35.

47 E. Klingelhofer, 'Vernacular architecture of the Munster Plantation'; the situation has recently improved with Colin Breen, *An Archaeology of Southwest Ireland* (Dublin, 2007).

48 R. F. Foster, *Modern Ireland 1600-1972* (New York, 1988), p. 59.

5

The archaeology of Kilcolman Castle

We are informed that at Kilcolman, the seat of this Seignory, there was a fair stone house built by Edmund Spencer [sic], which was utterly destroyed in the late wars; that the same, being re-edified, was lately consumed by fire. Since which time a convenient English house is built in the place thereof.

Survey of the Plantation of Munster, 1622[1]

The Elizabethan court poet Edmund Spenser, author of *The Faerie Queene* and colonial officer in County Cork, resided at Kilcolman Castle from around 1588 to October 1598, shortly before his death in January 1599.[2] Granted a 3000 acre estate by Elizabeth, Spenser repaired and improved the castle, a small medieval enclosure on a hilltop overlooking a marshy lake and bog. Its fate was to be burned and abandoned, then later used as a quarry for building stone. Archaeological fieldwork directed by the writer took place at Kilcolman from 1993 to 1996 to determine what evidence still existed for Spenser's occupancy of the castle. The project was sponsored by Mercer University and the Earthwatch Foundation, with support from University College Cork and the Royal Archaeological Institute.[3] The project located wall lines enclosing the 40m square castle bawn (or bailey) and identified four major buildings. These were the standing remains of a tower-house residence, the cellar or undercroft of a Great Hall, a service building (probably the kitchen), and a structure, identified as an Elizabethan parlour, that Spenser erected between the tower-house and the Great Hall.[4]

Spenser's life in Ireland, and at Kilcolman in particular, has long been of interest to literary scholars. The relevance of his residence to his poetry, however, is hotly contested, even when his ideological views of Elizabethan Ireland are not.[5] Such recent commentators as Andrew Hadfield have argued that 'Spenser had been in Ireland for (at least) ten years when he published the first edition of the *Faerie Queene* ... It would be strange if his Irish experience had not modified his sense of identity.'[6] Others, such as Christopher Burlinson, rejecting the New Historicism and the materialism it infers, see the potential value of the Kilcolman ruins quite differently than Thomas Herron, who draws from topography and archaeology in his Spenserian studies.[7] Yet Burlinson correctly observed that the Kilcolman excavations were not in search of Spenser's artistic imagination: they did not attempt to 'recover the creative experience of the poet'.[8] Upon reflection, archaeological interpretation here does try to establish an historical and material context for Spenser's activities and his ideas. But it cannot provide insight, only a setting, a frame, in which his art can be better viewed, perhaps by separating it from the distractions of the ensuing past and present.

The site (see Figure 5.1)

Kilcolman Castle lies on the southeastern slope of the east end of a short, low ridge, a typical formation in the undulating limestone of the Black-water River valley in north County Cork. Two miles south of the site flows the Awbeg rivulet, called by Spenser the 'Mulla', and equidistant to the north lie the modest Ballyhoura Mountains. Kilcolman Hill overlooks one of the wetlands now rare in County Cork, a small marsh or fen, with a little lake on the side close to the castle. Kilcolman Bog may have been

Figure 5.1 Aerial photo of Kilcolman Bog, 1994. The tower-house stands in the middle right, overlooking the oval-shaped bog dominating the foreground.

entirely a lake at the end of the last Ice Age. It remains an essential site for migrating Arctic wildfowl, and is an Irish wildlife refuge of international importance. The western end of the ridge contains a wide cavern, now largely blocked by stonefall (and occupied by badgers), but tradition has it extending far into the hill, which would be appropriate in limestone formations. The cave is also the basis for the fanciful account of a secret escape route by which Spenser, like Aeneas, led his family from the burning home.

The ruins of Kilcolman Castle have been the subject of several romantic depictions (of dubious accuracy), the most reliable of which was drawn by William Bartlett for his 1842 *Scenery and Antiquities of Ireland*[9] (see Figure 5.2). The site has been visited by antiquaries and men of letters, who commented upon the ruined tower-house, now standing only because of inelegant repairs made in the mid-nineteenth century by the Harold-Barry landowning family. One of the visitors, John Bernard Trotter, former secretary to the reforming MP Charles Fox, stopped by Kilcolman in a tour of Ireland:

> In a few moments Kilcolman-castle, a ruin of considerable magnitude, resting in lonely grandeur on the side of a small lake, rose before our eyes ...We stood transfixed to the spot many minutes. History unfurled her rich page before us; and in the mind's eye, with rapid glance, hurried over leading events of the glorious Elizabeth's reign, of which Edmund Spencer [*sic*] was the noblest ornament.[10]

A brief reconnaissance of the site in 1990 found Kilcolman Castle to comprise a late medieval tower-house, typical in design though of smaller size than many[11] (see Figure 5.3). Its accompanying bawn courtyard walls could be traced only in a few places along the south and east sides. At the southeast corner, standing masonry by a large depression suggested the site of a corner tower beside the cellar or undercroft to a medieval hall. Elsewhere along the crest of the ridge north of the tower-house, uneven ground under high grass hinted at possible earthworks and buried foundations.

Shortly before this, an important survey of Kilcolman Castle had been carried out by David Newman Johnson, architectural historian with the Office of Public Works. Johnson's work was thorough, in both field and file, resulting in a full account of the site's documentary and architectural histories published as the Kilcolman Castle entry in *The Spenser Encyclopedia*.[12] He made what observations were then possible, given thick vegetation on the ground and upon the walls of the tower-house, and he called for the removal of the structurally damaging ivy and for an

Figure 5.2 View of Kilcolman Castle, 1842.

Figure 5.3 Aerial photo of Kilcolman tower-house, 1994.

archaeological investigation of the site. The subsequent fieldwork undertaken by the writer was partially in response to Johnson's appeal.

Summary of fieldwork at Kilcolman Castle (see Figure 5.4)

Fieldwork at Kilcolman began in 1993 with the unrewarding but necessary task of clearing vegetation from the site and ivy from the walls of the tower-house, followed by a contour survey of the adjacent hillside and the start of a three-year geophysical survey of the castle vicinity, using soil resistivity metering equipment from University College Cork. At the same time, specialists in historic architectural preservation undertook a detailed architectural survey of the tower-house, incorporating the details newly exposed from the plant cover. In 1994, excavation units received letter identifications in the order in which they were opened up: three trenches that year, inside the tower-house (A), between it and the

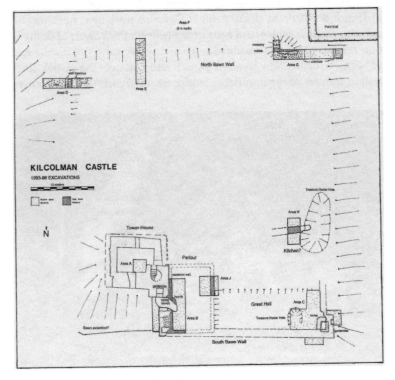

Figure 5.4 Kilcolman Castle, plan of excavations.

standing masonry of the bawn (bailey) wall to the south (B), and at the presumed hall at the southeast corner of the castle (C). Trench A was quickly completed. There, traces of an early cobbled floor survived under Victorian reworking of the vaulted-ceiling ground floor room. Trenches B and C revealed unexpectedly deep and complex stratigraphies. In Trench B, the team found that a late seventeenth-century cottage had been built in the ruins of the castle, and in Trench C, the ground had been previously dug into by modern treasure hunters and by Georgian labourers quarrying for the well-dressed stones on wall surfaces. There, nearly two metres of rubble and infilled soils were excavated without finding a floor. One 1990 assumption proved correct; a small tower had been added to the southeast corner of the castle. This proved to have served more physical than military needs, because it housed a garderobe (privy) that served the Great Hall.

The strategy for the 1995 season was to locate the general lines of the bawn enclosure and to continue working out the complex stratigraphy of Trench B, where the clearing out of Victorian workmen's trenches had revealed exciting evidence of a major fire beneath thick layers of destruction rubble, which was assumed to be archaeological proof for the end of Spenser's castle. New trenches D, E, F, and G sought the castle's outer wall in features of the immediate landscape. In Trench G a short length

Figure 5.5 Kilcolman Castle, excavation of north bawn wall, from west.

of the 1.85m (5 feet) wide north bawn wall was uncovered (see Figure 5.5). Elsewhere it had been completely dismantled, but one could observe traces of clay soils used to level up the ground surface beneath it and in the rubble fill of the wall's core between two faces of laid stones. Close to the east bawn wall, Trench H examined masonry that had been smashed through by a large treasure hunter's hole, which was probably machine-made from the 1970s or 1980s. The excavation exposed a 0.95m (3 feet) wide wall running at right angles to the line of the east bawn wall. Its upper courses had been rebuilt, not using mortar like the original wall, but with a clay bonding. This wall runs in the direction of the tower-house, and it probably served double duty in defining an inner and outer bailey and in forming one side of what may have been a kitchen wing off the eastern, 'lower' end of the medieval Great Hall. The Hall's 'upper' end would have been closer to the family's personal accommodations in the tower-house.

The final season saw Trench B reach the pre-Spenserian strata, Trench C hit floor level and construction phase, and Trench J (the letter I was not used) examine the connection between the two buildings revealed by trenches B and C. In Trench B, the team excavated ash and burnt timbers found *in situ* beneath the collapsed walls of a building identified as a Tudor 'parlour' between the Great Hall and the residential tower-house

Figure 5.6 Kilcolman Castle, excavation of 'Parlour' destruction, burned timbers.

Figure 5.7 Kilcolman Castle, excavation of Great Hall garderobe, from northwest.

block (see Figure 5.6). Ground-floor parlours would become so common that most seventeenth-century gentry families took their meals there or in a first-floor dining-room.[13] Often using earlier, mortared walls as foundations, the walls of this structure had fine white plaster surfaces covering a clay-bonded masonry. A rare find, a nearly complete clay tobacco pipe discovered among the burnt debris, proved to be a type typical of the early 1600s but not of the Elizabethan period. This important clue demonstrated that the fire was not that of 1598, when Edmund and his family fled to the safety of the walls of Cork city. Rather, it was the fire recorded as having caused Sylvanus Spenser to abandon the castle and by *ca.*1620 erect an English-style manor house on the estate, as recorded in the survey quoted at the head of this chapter. Following his father's death, Sylvanus reoccupied and refurbished Kilcolman, probably after the 1601 Battle of Kinsale solidified English control of Munster. The damaged remains of Edmund's Parlour were discovered under Sylvanus's raised floor levels and rebuilt chimney hearth. To preserve these layers for future archaeology, only a small area was excavated. It suggested that the construction of Spenser's Parlour was tied to a major rebuilding of the castle, corroborating the claim that the castle was derelict when he acquired it, probably the result of the Desmond wars of the 1570s and 1580s.

The excavation in Trench C established a sequence of construction phases. The fact that the walls had been constructed near bog level at the base of the hill, not on its crest or slope, continued to have only one logical explanation: they had enclosed a large storage cellar under a Great Hall built above it along the southern bawn wall. Around the end of the Middle Ages, the cellar was deliberately filled with several feet of compact soil, apparently to remedy the natural dampness, while a small garderobe tower was built at the southeast corner, its waste chute emptying to the east, presumably away from the windows of the Great Hall. Problems with dampness must have remained a concern, because a sump was soon cut inside the southeast corner, beneath the tower (see Figure 5.7). The material raising the cellar floor level contained much ironworking debris, presumably from a castle forge. Destruction fills here yielded a rare artifact perhaps associated with Spenser the poet: a lute peg, an ivory or bone tuning pin for an early stringed instrument, worn down where the attached string was adjusted[14] (see Figure 5.12).

Progress achieved in Trench C permitted the excavation of an additional unit, Trench J, at the junction of the Great Hall and the Parlour. In the remaining days of the final field season, excavators removed upper layers to expose structural features. Uppermost was part of a later cottage, also found in Trench B, which was built in the castle ruins and here covered over the intact plastered faces of the Spenser walls at a higher level than in Trench B. Clearly much of the Spenser home has been preserved at Kilcolman. Trench J revealed the line of the Elizabethan Parlour's east wall, beneath which was found a portion of the west wall of the medieval cellar. Completing the project, the architectural survey was brought up to date, integrating masonry in the standing ruins with the discoveries below ground.

Spenser's life at Kilcolman

What, then, was the appearance of Kilcolman while Spenser lived there? Contemporary writings help recreate the physical structures that housed the various functions of the castle.

Barnaby Googe, who spent much time in Ireland, translated and added to the German *Foure Bookes of Husbandry*, in which he describes the service buildings around a functional manor's courtyard. The residence itself is:

> built with Galeries and Gables, as it both receiveth the Sunne in Winter, and the shadowe in Sommer: besides, you have a fayre Porche as you enter in, that keepeth away the wind and the rayne from the doore. [The house] is commodiously & handsomely placed ... upon a higher ground both for the safeguard of the foundation, and for the better ayre and fayrer prospect: beside, my Garden and my Orchard are adjoyning to it, which with the sweete smell of the floures, and the fayre beautie of the trees, bringeth both health and pleasure.

In the courtyard,

> buildings severed from the rest, doo serve for gheste chambers, with a chamber for my hotte house ... These offices (for feare of fyre) you see, are all severed from the house: there is hereunto adjoining a very fayre well, which besides the service here, dooth also serve my Kitchin and other houses of office ...
>
> Over my Gate I have laid my Steward, from whence he may look into the Court, and to the Gate, and oversee his neighbour the Bayly ... Over-agaynst the gate, as you see, at the South side of the Court, there is a back-house [bakehouse], and a Cornemill, ... and a Pastrie with two Ovens, one serving for household bread, the other for manchet for myne own table, and for Tartes and fine baakemeates. Here are also Troughes to keep meale in, and troughes to lay leaven in, and there is a fayre table to mould upon ..., there is also a Brewehouse with an Oast for drying of Malt to make Beere with.

Elsewhere:

> You see a voyd roome before the Kitchin, whiche is an entrie both to the Kitchin, to the folkes Chamber, and to the Oxhouses ... The Kiching is ... so well pargetted the rooffe ... because I have a great number of serantes, which for lacke of other roome, doo dine and suppe here: besides, the pargetting or seeling, is a good safetie against fyre ... Here is a good handsome rooffe by the Chimney, well stored with redde Hearing, Bacon, and Martilmas beefe, there is also a handsome sinke by the Kitchin. Hereunto is also joined my Larder, a vault with three rooms, one serving for Butter and Milke, the other for Beere and Wine, the third for to keepe fleshe in. Above in the loft yonder, doo I lay my Corne upon a fayre floore, closely fenced and seeled against Mise ... Harde by, is another loft very close ... serving for my fruite.

On the 'backside' of the house:

> On each side, are lodginges for my servantes, and other roomes and loftes for strawe and fodder for my cattel; and there by the stables, are also servantes lodginges on every side, and my maides chamber neere the Kitchin, and the wasshing house.[15]

Googe is describing a manor house that is the centre of a working estate, whilst Kilcolman was a castle, albeit a small one. Spenser's letter to Raleigh refers to it as 'my house at Kilcolman', which ought to be taken to read 'home' rather than 'house', just as Book II, Canto IX, of his *Faerie Queene* concerns 'The House of Temperance, in which / Doth sober Alma dwell'. This building, an allegory of the human body, is not actually a house, but 'a goodly castle, placed / Foreby a river in a pleasant dale'. Details comprise the castle gate, protected by a barbican and portcullis, and the 'castle wall, / that was so high as foe might not it climb, / And all so fair and fensible withal-' though made of clay. Inside, 'she them brought into a stately hall, / Wherein were many tables fair dispread, / And ready dight with drapets festival, / Against the viands should be ministered.'

At the upper end was the steward, who directed the marshal in disposing of 'both guests and meat'. Alma showed the guests the kitchen and finally the parlour:

> It was a vault y-built for great dispense,
> With many ranges reared along the wall,
> And one great chimney ...
> ... fair Alma led them right,
> And soon into a goodly parlor brought,
> That was with royal arras richly dight,...
> And in the midst thereof upon the floor,

A lovely bevy of fair ladies sate,
... Soone as the gracious Alma came in place,
They all attonce out of their seates arose,
And to her homage made, with humble grace:
... Till that great Ladie thence away them sought,
to view her castles other wondrous frame.
Up to a stately Turret she them brought,
Ascending by ten steps of Alabaster wrought[16]

Spenser's Kilcolman was still largely a late medieval Irish castle, of the 'tower-house and bawn' variety. Walls would have been of stone, either mortar or clay bonded, and possibly whitewashed, with the finer interior rooms plastered and perhaps panelled or tapestried; it possibly had plank floors and panelled ceilings. Service floors would have been earthen with disposable rushes to collect dirt, or of beaten clay or cobbling, though one floor tile fragment was recovered. No stone or tile roofing was found, so roofs would have been made of wooden shingles or thatch. The tower-house could well have had a floor level above the surviving walls, although there is no evidence for an upper vault to support it. Indeed floor joists spanning the tower-house at the present top floor level would have provided space for occupants of that storey, and the upper passage over the entrance doorway, instead of leading to a further flight of stairs, could have served a projecting machicolation to protect the entrance (see Figure 5.8). The stair tower at the southeast corner of the tower-house was the result of a major rebuilding, probably to insert the well-appointed garderobe room and its shaft. It is possible that both garderobes were added at the same time, in an 'updating the plumbing' project, probably a generation before Spenser's residency.

The wide circuit of the bawn wall is also likely to have stood during the Spenser period, enclosing a space roughly 40m (125 feet) square. It would have been perhaps 3.5 metres (twelve feet) high, thickened at the base with an angled batter (see Figure 5.9). The bawn gate most likely lay west of the tower-house, where a 'hollow way' cuts down the hillside toward an ancient roadway skirting the bog at this point, reminding us that the castle faced south, toward the bogside road and the Awbeg, and away from the thickly wooded Ballyhoura mountains. Evidence for new construction on older foundations should be ascribed to Spenser; the centre of a busy estate of over 3000 acres would need a number of service buildings, such as stable, barn, forge, cart shed, well house, storage rooms, kitchen, servants' lodging, etc. It is likely that the northern half of the bawn contained gardens, and one may conjecture that the east side near the presumed kitchen was reserved for vegetables and that a knot garden lay to the west, where it could be viewed from the tower-house.[17]

As the seat of a seignory, or lordship, Kilcolman had administrative and ceremonial functions appropriate to an open hall, which a man of substance would normally use for feeding and entertaining dependants and friends, as well as for dispensing manorial justice.[18] Although the north wall of the structure identified as the Great Hall lay outside the excavated area, a reasonable width would be half the length, which gives internal measurements of 16m x 8m (52 by 26 feet).[19] The structure identified as the Parlour measured 10m x 6.5m (35 by 22 feet), and floor joists

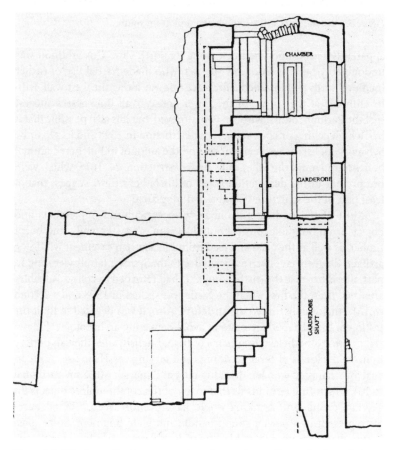

Figure 5.8 Kilcolman Castle, cross section of tower-house. Drawn by Irene Jackson Henry.

Figure 5.9 Kilcolman Castle, south bawn wall, from south.

apparently rested upon bedrock along its north side. This addition was undoubtedly built by Edmund Spenser, who made partial use of earlier medieval walls and installed a fireplace midway along the west wall, with its chimney at the corner of the tower-house. Wall thicknesses suggest that the Parlour could have been two-storeyed, but it is also possible that it had a high ceiling or open rafters. Its destruction in 1598 and its repair by Sylvanus Spenser is well evidenced, and the amount of butchered animal bones found amid the ashes of its final destruction, *ca.* 1615, which were not present in the destruction levels of his father's time, suggest that at least part of the structure served as a dining area.

Most of the finds at Kilcolman were agricultural implements and objects from building construction, like stones, plaster, nails, and burnt timber, as well as the glass and lead from Elizabethan casement windows; artifacts likely to have been associated with the Spenser family were few. In part, this is because the castle occupants had returned to collect valuables after two fires, the first when the castle was sacked in 1598 and a second *ca.*1615 that finally ruined the structure. Also, it was decided to limit the testing of the Elizabethan strata to avoid damaging archaeological material *in situ*. Nonetheless, fragments of Irish, English, and Rhenish pottery indicate the kinds of ceramic storage and serving vessels in use. A medieval four-handled wooden drinking mug at Limerick Museum attributed to Kilcolman Bog reminds us that many of the commonplace objects for serving, eating, and drinking would have been of treen.[20] Metal wares were present in a pewter spoon handle and plate fragment. Some glass had melted into unidentifiable lumps, but glass vessels in general were rare at Kilcolman. Among personal items were pins, a spur, the bronze tip to a knife scabbard, and metal fittings for furniture or trunks, along with the above-mentioned clay tobacco pipes and bone lute peg (see Figures 5.10, 5.11, 5.12). To these finds can be added the remains of plants and animals, from which we can make some observations on the diet of the Spenser family at Kilcolman. It should be noted that only a limited portion of the site was excavated, and that samples were small and the conclusions drawn from them are tenuous.

The animal bone assemblage from Kilcolman Castle was judged a typical domestic sample and included remains that suggest the slaughter, preparation, and consumption of domestic livestock within the castle.[21] The material is characterized by a high frequency of sheep (or goat), and it is clear that mutton and occasionally lamb played an important dietary role. By fragment count and number of individuals present, sheep was the most prominent species represented, with cattle occupying a secondary place. Pig remains were extremely scarce, indicating that pork was only occasionally served. The faunal sample included a small number of remains from red deer and rabbit. Rabbits may have been kept in cages within the castle or as wild specimens living in a warren on the estate. The deer bones could represent the results of hunting excursions, a popular sport among the elite. Bird bones were few, and domestic fowl seemed to be the only commonly eaten avian species: some bantams and a few probably prized chickens. Other birds eaten at Kilcolman were duck and a small species of wild goose, probably Brent goose. Shellfish also seem to have been a favored food item as evidenced by the recovery of oyster shells from many contexts in the Parlour and kitchen.

To understand the husbandry system that produced animals whose remains were studied, one must consider the age of the animals at death. The faunal evidence suggests a local husbandry with sheep as the most important animals, followed by cattle and then swine. The importance of sheep as reflected in the archaeological record from Cork City sites of the late sixteenth and early seventeenth centuries has parallels here. Cork was an important centre for the wool trade during the post-medieval period and the ageing evidence from various excavated sites there suggests a husbandry whose main aim was the production of wool for the European market. The majority of sheep from Kilcolman Castle were kept until they were at least three years of age, apparently following a local husbandry system that was primarily aimed at producing wool. Thus, Edmund Spenser's estate appears to have been integrated into the southern Irish market economy that began in the late medieval period and rapidly grew under the Tudors.

The Kilcolman Castle material has also produced some information

Figure 5.10 Metal finds from Kilcolman Castle. From top: copper alloy (bronze) tip or chape for a knife scabbard; copper alloy (brass) pin; fragment of lead alloy (pewter) plate.

about the culinary preparations and preferences of its Elizabethan inhabitants, though it is difficult to make a firm statement about the level of prosperity of the occupants, given the small size of the sample. Many specimens were totally blackened as though they had been in contact with fire for some time, but not long enough for the bones to become totally calcined. This type of damage probably occurred while joints of meat were being spit roasted over a large open fireplace. The red deer

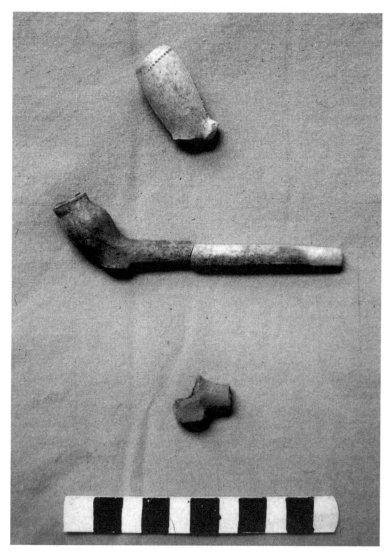

Figure 5.11 Tobacco pipes from Kilcolman Castle. From top: white clay pipe bowl fragment, second half of seventeenth century; intact white clay (stained) pipe bowl with part of stem, from the 1620s to 1630s; fragment of red clay pipe bowl, probably made in Co. Cork, later seventeenth century.

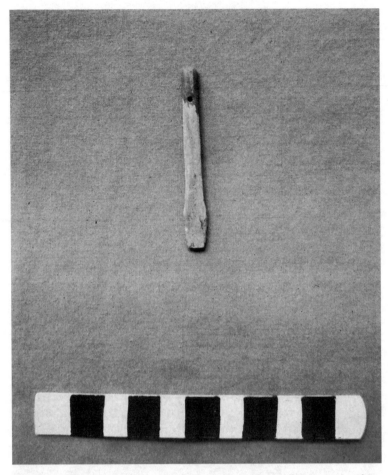

Figure 5.12 Bone tuning peg of a lute or similar stringed instrument, from Kilcolman Castle.

remains together with the fish and oyster shells indicate high status foods, appropriate for the inhabitants of a castle. The presence of oyster shells and marine fish species at Kilcolman Castle does point to a certain degree of wealth and status, as these food items would have been transported a considerable distance from the coast. In addition to these 'elite' animals, a certain richness in the food waste is also suggested by a relatively high species variety and animals having been slaughtered at a young age. The differences between this assemblage and contemporary urban sites are slight, however, and it cannot be argued that the inhabitants had a living standard far above that of dwellers in post-medieval Cork, for instance. Both assemblages are dominated by cattle and sheep, and the age groups that are represented indicate that wool and hide production was significant for both.

Plant remains were found in soil samples collected from the ashy destruction layer of the Parlour, which had already yielded some carbonized plant remains, and from the castle's main cesspit below the tower-house garderobe chute.[22] Wheat, barley, oats, and rye were all found at the site, though the quantities of plant remains recovered were too small to say which of the cereals were dominant on the entire site. Broadwheats certainly dominated the sample from the tower-house cesspit, and this may be considered a prestige cereal, as it produces a higher quality flour. Oats were present in two samples, but some or all could have been grown for animal consumption. The absence of chaff also prevents identification of the exact type of oats present. It is possible that the charred seeds are *Avena fatua* (wild oat), and thus represent the weed component of a crop. Because wild oat grains are the same size and weight as domestic grains, they are difficult to remove from a harvested crop by both traditional methods (winnowing and sieving) and modern mechanized crop processing.

The general picture we have of the medieval Irish agricultural economy is that the cereal component was dominated by oats. They are found in most productive samples and were used for both human and animal consumption. Oats dominate in rural (e.g. Barryscourt, Co. Cork) and urban contexts, both towns (Athenry, Co. Galway) and cities (Waterford and Cork). Other cereals were important, especially after the arrival of the Anglo-Normans, when the agricultural economy moved to a market basis. Recent work at Barryscourt, Co. Cork, and Dunamase, Co. Laois, appear to have discovered storage contexts in which oats dominated the assemblages. The late Elizabethan period, however, would have seen a change in demand for a more English type of diet.

Given the high social status of the castle occupants and in the case of the Spenser family, their English cultural background, it was hoped that a wider range of plant foodstuffs would be found. Unfortunately, no spices, fruits, or indeed pulses (legumes) were identified. It is probable that the main reasons for this are taphonomic. Pulses do not require exposure to heat as part of their processing and are consequently difficult to find in the archaeological record. Similarly, vegetables are grossly under-represented, especially as they should be harvested before they produce seeds. They are usually visible only in waterlogged preservation conditions and require more specialized methods of recovery and analysis.

The types of food eaten on sites like Kilcolman are usually known from documentary sources, which reveal social and cultural differences in diet. Fynes Moryson mentioned that the cultural background of the town dwellers affected their diet, as 'many of the English Irish have by little and little been infected with the Irish filthiness, and that, in Waterford, they more retain the English diet'.[23] Edmund Spenser himself referred to cultural differences when he described the Gaelic practice of booleying 'to live in herds, driving their cattle continually with them and feeding only on their milk and white meats'.[24]

As the grains found at Kilcolman were charred, it follows that they had *not* been eaten. Presumably they were charred accidentally in food preparation, crop processing, or in accidental fires. The grains could have been used for the preparation of breads, gruels, or alcoholic beverages. As none of the grains contained sprouted embryos, they cannot be associated with the practice of brewing, which was common on Irish estates. Malting involves soaking grains until they begin to sprout, then arresting the sprout by exposure to hot air; high proportions of sprouted grains can be indicators of malting. Luke Gernon's 1620 *Discourse on Ireland* provides a quaint description of the range of drinks offered to travelers at a castle:

> You shall be presented with all the drinks in the house, first the ordinary beer, then aquavitae, then sack, then old ale. The Lady tastes it, you must not refuse it. In the morning there will be brought to you a cup of aquavitae. [U]squebath of Ireland is not such an extraction as it is made in England, but far more qualified and sweetened with licorish. When you are disposing yourself to depart, you are again presented with all the drinks in the house as at your first entrance. Smack them over and depart.[25]

Findings

The excavations at Kilcolman Castle produced valuable clues to life among the colonial elite in Elizabethan Ireland as well as tantalizing hints of what archaeological evidence remains to be discovered. The southern half of the castle bawn enclosure was filled with buildings: a four-storey residential tower-house for family and retainers, a Great Hall with infilled cellar, an Elizabethan Parlour, and a kitchen with other service buildings. The absence of identifiable building remains within the northern part of the bawn circuit suggests that it was the site of the castle gardens. Presumably, a kitchen garden lay to the east near the service buildings and kitchen, and a pleasure garden lay to the west where it could be viewed from the residential tower-house. Recovered artifacts and ecofacts do speak of the Spenser family's daily life: sights and sounds, smells and tastes may be inferred, respectively, by window panes, a lute peg, tobacco pipes, and a diet that included fine bread, shellfish, and a broad variety of meats.

Faunal and plant analysis indicate a way of life at Kilcolman, as expected, superior to that of the contemporary Irish population. Yet the Spenser family may have lived more like the Irish aristocratic and merchant classes than the English educated, courtier class. Game, seafood, younger meat animals, and white bread were part of the diet, but the limited sampling cannot determine how exceptional or how typical they were. Future archaeological research at Kilcolman Castle will undoubtedly answer these and other questions about life at Edmund Spenser's home. For the present, we can suggest that the economy of the Kilcolman estate was likely that of a mixed agricultural regime, supporting a diet that included a regular use of some foodstuffs not locally produced. Sheep and cattle were raised for wool and hides, then slaughtered and eaten on the estate. The commonplace oats were present, but the lighter breadwheats preferred by the elite were also grown locally. Meals of rabbit, venison, and seafood drew from the prestige foods of both rural aristocracy and urban elite. The Spenser family enjoyed household utensils and a diet roughly similar to what they would have had in the English countryside, and one that was equal to that of the wealthy Irish. For many settlers, colonial Munster may not have offered all the comforts of an English home, but for Edmund Spenser, this Englishman's home was quite literally his castle.

Notes

1 *State Papers Ireland Eliz.*, 144, No. 14; Kilcolman entry is reproduced on pp. 143–4 in R. Dunlop, 'An unpublished survey of the Plantation of Munster in 1622', *J. Royal Soc. Antiquaries of Ireland*, 54 (1924), pp. 128–46.

2 Although much improved by scholars since, Pauline Henley's *Spenser in Ireland* (Cork and London, 1928) is the seminal work on Spenser's later residency. Neville Williams supplies interesting background information on Spenser's contacts at Court and his 'banishment' to Ireland in *All the Queen's Men: Elizabeth I and her Courtiers* (London 1972, repr.1974), pp. 163–5.

3 It should be noted that among the eighty-something Earthwatch volunteers from 1993 to 1996 at Kilcolman Castle were two Spenserians – Sheila Cavanagh of Emory University and Richard Berlith of St Francis College. The latter's second edition of *The Twilight Lords: Elizabeth I and the Plunder of Ireland* (New York, 2002) offers 'Afterword 2000: Spenser at Kilcolman', pp. 295–318, with insightful reflections on excavation experiences and the poet's residency at Kilcolman.

4 The excavation results have been published: E. Klingelhofer, 'Edmund Spenser at Kilcolman Castle: the archaeological evidence', *Post-Medieval Archaeol.* 39 (2005), pp.135–54. The complete report and site archive is deposited with the Department of Ancient Monuments, Office of Public Works, Dublin.

5 See W. Maley, *Salvaging Spenser: Colonialism, Culture and Identity* (London, 1997).

6 Andrew Hadfield, *Edmund Spenser's Irish Experience: Wilde Fruit and Salvage Soil* (Oxford, 1997) p. 129.

7 Christopher Burlinson, *Allegory, Space and the Material World in the Writings of Edmund Spenser* (Cambridge, 2006); Thomas Herron, 'Irish den of thieves: souterrains (and a crannog) in Books V and VI of Spenser's *Faerie Queene*' *Spenser Studies* 14 (2000), pp. 303–17.

8 Burlinson, *Allegory, Space and the Material World*, pp. 160–3.

9 W. H. Bartlett, *Scenery and Antiquities of Ireland*, vol. 2 (London, 1842).

10 John Bernard Trotter (private secretary to the late Right Hon. C. J. Fox), *Walks through Ireland in the Years 1812, 1814, and 1817* (London, 1819) p. 286.

11 Changing observations based on developing fieldwork were reported by E. Klingelhofer to the International Spenser Society, first 'The archaeology of Kilcolman Castle: preliminary observations', Western Michigan University, 1991; then 'The archaeology of Kilcolman Castle', Yale University, 1996; and lastly 'Kilcolman Castle: past and future archaeology', University of Toronto, 2006.

12 D. N. Johnson, 'Kilcolman Castle', in A. C. Hamilton (ed.), *The Spenser Encyclopedia* (Toronto, 1990), pp. 417–22.

13 J. T. Cliffe, *The World of the Country House in the Seventeenth-Century* (New Haven and London, 1999), p. 28.

14 Archaeologist Carter Hudgins was able to identify the object immediately because he had found twenty-four similar pegs in his own excavation of the burned ruins of early eighteenth-century Corotoman mansion in Virginia, for which, see *The King's Realm: Archaeology at Robert's Carter's Corotoman* (forthcoming). Contemporary information on lutes may be found in R. Dowland, *Varietie of Lute-lessons* (London, 1610; repr. Amsterdam, 1969). See also, M. Spring, *The Lute in Britain: A History of the Instrument and its Music* (Oxford, 2001), and R. Berlith, *Twilight Lords*, pp. 295–6, who reminds us that it was he who unearthed the artifact, a most appropriate discovery for a Spenser enthusiast.

15 B. Googe, *Foure Books of Husbandry, collected by M. Conradus Heresbachus ... Newely Englished, and increased, by Barnabe Googe, Esquire* (London, 1577; repr. Amsterdam, 1971), pp. 9–12; for Googe and Ireland, see E. M. Horton, *Ireland through Tudor Eyes* (Philadelphia, 1935), p. 32.

16 E. Spenser, *Fairie Queene: Book Two*, E. Greenlaw (ed.), (Baltimore, 1933), pp. 112, 115–19, 121.

17 For a possible garden at Kilcolman, see Klingelhofer, 'Edmund Spenser at Kilcolman', pp. 143–4. Excavations at a contemporary Munster tower-house, Barryscourt Castle, may have located garden planting and bedding features: D. Pollock, 'The bawn exposed', in J. Ludlow and N. Jameson (eds), *Medieval Ireland: The Barryscourt Lectures I-X* (Kinsale, 2004), p. 167. For knot, or 'emblematic' gardens, see R. C. Strong, *The Renaissance Garden in England* (London, 1979), p.10.

18 Although Renaissance-minded aristocrats were abandoning the traditional Great Hall, there is reason to believe that the gentry were not so inclined. See C. King, 'Organization of social spaces in late medieval manor houses: an East Anglian study', *Archaeol. J.* 160 (2003), pp. 125–59, esp. p.121.

19 The average 2:1 ratio of dimensions and the comparative measurements of halls, are found in M. Wood, *The English Medieval House* (London, 1965), pp. 64–5.

20 Limerick Museum reports that the *mether* has a note of provenance attributing it to Kilcolman, though not necessarily 'four leather water-bottles of Cromwellian type'

stored with it (Larry Walsh, pers. comm.). See J. W. Waterer, 'Leather objects of interest in the Limerick Museum', *North Munster Ant. J.*, 10, (1966), pp. 78–9, pl. 4.

21 The discussion of animal bones is taken from M. McCarthy, 'Faunal remains', in Klingelhofer, 'Edmund Spenser at Kilcolman', pp. 148, 150–1.

22 The discussion of plant remains is based on J. Tierney , 'Plant remains', in Klingelhofer, 'Edmund Spenser at Kilcolman', pp. 148–9, 151–2.

23 F. Moryson, 'An itinerary'(1617) , in C. L. Falkiner (ed.), *Illustrations of Irish History, Mainly of the Seventeenth Century* (London, 1904), pp. 211–309.

24 E. Spenser, 'View of the state of Ireland', pp. 503–56 in H. J. Todd (ed.), *The Works of Edmund Spenser* (London, 1884); for boolying, see pp. 552–3.

25 L. Gernon, 'A discourse of Ireland', in Falkiner, *Illustrations of Irish History* , pp. 345–62.

6

Spenserian architecture in Ireland

Alas all the Castles I have, are built with ayre, thou know'st.

Ben Jonson, 1605[1]

Ben Jonson's comedy *Eastward Ho* reveals how the early seventeenth century still valued castles as important social possessions. The claim by an impecunious Sir Petronell to have a castle and estate, more than his title, attracted the social-climbing daughter of the rich goldsmith Touchstone. For purely military purposes, castles had become obsolete with successful French siege artillery in Normandy and Gascony nearly 200 years earlier. During the 1540s Henry VIII erected coastal artillery forts as 'castles', but after that the term was little used by the English military.[2] One could thus assume that Jonson employed an archaic idiom for dramatic effect, were it not for the fact that structures termed 'castles' were still being built in both England and Ireland. The small, late medieval tower-house castle continued to appear in late sixteenth- and early seventeenth-century Ireland, but it was being steadily replaced by the fortified house. In England, some older castles may have been called upon to play a role in the power politics of the western and northern borderlands, but most of the nobility preferred to reside in undefended manor houses. The latter offered the owner prestige in its traditional or Renaissance decorations, comfort in its new uses of space, and even security by not posing a threat to the suspicious and ruthless Tudor monarchs. Yet late in Elizabeth's reign and well into James's, some members of the elite chose to erect what they termed 'castles', structures superficially fortified in a style that has been labelled 'Spenserian' after the poet of Elizabethan chivalry, Edmund Spenser. The question posed here is whether the continued tradition of defended residences in Ireland was related to this English 'chivalric revival' in aristocratic architecture. Moreover, the houses built by the elite in Ireland during the Plantation Period no doubt projected power and status, but a firmer understanding of this elite depends upon whether they saw themselves as a colonial or an imperial ruling class.[3]

Elizabethan architecture

The major architectural development in England from the fifteenth to the seventeenth centuries was the nearly universal conversion of elite residences from medieval halls to Tudor or Stuart mansions.[4] Within these centuries, there were various influences, impulses, and sudden bursts of construction, which can be traced to the effects of changes in royal policy and to families' access to power in the ever-growing nation state. The Tudor dynasty itself witnessed and intermittently embraced the arrival of Renaissance architectural elements into northern Europe. Ambitious experiments like the royal tombs in Westminster Abbey and the flamboyant Nonsuch Palace were financed by Henry VII and VIII, but a broader impetus for architectural innovation seems not to have taken place until political culture and social change created a mid-sixteenth-century 'classical moment' of self-fashioning by the new Tudor courtier class.[5] A strong Gothic tradition, however, took post-Perpendicular forms in such features as staircases and bay windows. Two late medieval trends, the widespread application of battlements and the growth in number or size of towers, received a 'pull' by the stylish castellations appearing in France and the Low Countries (disseminated in Books of Hours) and a 'push' by the need for security against the level of lawlessness reported in the late fifteenth-century Paston family letters.[6] Noble residences became multi-unit affairs, with ranges of lodging around courts that focused on overlarge, keep-like towers like Tattershall and Ashby-de-la-Zouche, or massive gatehouse towers like Kirby Muxloe, old Hatfield, Hampton Court, and Christ College, Cambridge[7] (see Figure 6.1). The last three were constructed by ecclesiastics, but served as prestigious residences, not religious centres. They may have had some Renaissance ornamentation, like the rondels at Hampton Court, but the overall format was essentially late medieval.

G. W. Hoskins proposed that the majority of English manor houses were transformed from medieval open-hall types into essentially modern plans with chimneys, hall/parlour divisions and upper bedrooms during the eighty-year period from 1560 to 1640.[8] Acknowledging the serious reservations of Matthew Johnson and others about the extent and chronology of Hoskins's thesis,[9] one could nevertheless suggest that a surge of new house construction on a large scale does indeed represent a 'Great'

Figure 6.1 Tattershall Castle keep, Lincolnshire, *ca.* 1450.

Rebuilding. In a different context and with a twist to the term 'great', one could point to the number of large-scale constructions by which 'Great' and 'near-Great' families remade their personal environments.[10] Part of the lengthy development of evolving residential architecture, this rebuilding and new building was given movement and direction by the social and economic changes of new wealth, new families, and new conditions.[11] Enough structures appeared in the period *ca.*1540 to *ca.*1640 – and have survived – to suggest what types of architecture were employed by the Tudor–Stuart elite. During the course of that century, architectural forms preferred by the upper class of England fell into three discernible styles: what has been called 'Tudor domestic Gothic'[12] but may be better referred to as 'traditional Tudor', another that emphasized classicism, and a third that promoted a chivalric image. This last Timothy Mowl called neo-medieval, but in reference to the social system it recalled, could be more strictly defined as neo-feudal.[13]

Several examples serve to illustrate this tripartite development and the forms that it took. Representative of a 'traditional Tudor' style is The Vyne in Hampshire, the seat of the Sandys family, courtiers who could boast of having three times entertained Henry VIII there (see Figure 6.2). The lively brick diapering survives from the original decorative scheme, which was maintained through later alterations, one of which converted the central tower into a gabled porch.[14] Renaissance classicism is associated with the Cecil family of William, Lord Burghley, and his son Robert, Earl of Salisbury, whose service to and rewards from the Crown pushed them into the highest ranks of the nobility[15] (see Figure 6.3). William Cecil used his residences of Theobalds and Burghley House to illustrate his dominant position at Elizabeth's court. Beginning the construction of Hatfield House in 1608, Robert Cecil's allegiance to and mastery of the Jacobean state took form in the classical motifs used in the rich woodwork dominating the interior. Outside, the facade of classical mass and regularity rises above Cardinal Wolsey's nearby brick palace, reduced to an ancillary function while retaining its medieval arrangement of hall, solar, and porch tower. Exuding even more classicism, Montacute House, *ca.* 1600, marked the Phelips family's rise on the national scene. As Speaker of the House of Commons, Sir Edward Phelips completed the wide-windowed east front where statues, niches, and round windows are complemented by a formal garden enclosed by exuberant balustrades and pavilions (see Figure 6.4).

Long after Cardinal Wolsey's overly ambitious Hampton Court construction, architecture as political statement continued in the series of

Figure 6.2 The Vyne, Hampshire, *ca.* 1520.

grand country houses erected by leading figures at Court. The intent was to display the reflected greatness of the monarch, a point directed as much to Elizabeth and James as to rising members of the national elite. In this tradition were the Cecils' three mansions, Christopher Hatton's Kirby Hall, and Bess Cavendish's new Hardwick Hall, all places where the monarch could be suitably received and would continue to 'hold court' in grand style.[16] These massive structures use space differently, but all contain Renaissance details and lack the martial elements evident

Figure 6.3 Burghley House, Huntingdonshire, *ca.* 1587.

elsewhere.[17] Such buildings signaled a desire to follow up on the early Tudor interest in Italian and French forms and decoration, but it was a message that also evoked the power of the early modern state to ensure law and order. These houses are defenceless; the Crown was their defence. It was also the source of their builders' status: three privy councillors and a lady-in-waiting erected the examples above. Show-houses celebrated their owners' success through several avenues: the law, bureaucracy, and even entertainment (Hatton's dancing charmed Elizabeth), but most importantly, *none* had a military background. Like their counterparts in

Figure 6.4 Garden facade of Montacute House, Somerset, *ca.* 1595.

France, the new generations of nobility more often had their origins in 'the robe' than in 'the sword'. In England, the civil elite expressed their status and sophistication by using classical decoration. The martial gentry and nobility displayed their power in castellated forms.

Spenserian architecture

Castles reappear in the English countryside with the third architectural style, which is not found before the last decades of Elizabeth's reign and seems not to have continued beyond the life of her successor, James I. The late sixteenth-century Chivalric Revival in general was part of the heightened social differentiation of late Renaissance courts, which revelled in such works as Ariosto's *Orlando Furioso* (1516). In England it may have been taken further than elsewhere. Dedicated to Elizabeth, Spenser's *Faerie Queene* embodied the cult of Gloriana, but also spoke to the English victories over religious enemies like the Armada and the conquest of Ireland. Elizabethan culture required an explanation for virtue and vigour in a state headed by a female. Does it stretch the evidence to suggest that chivalric castellation flourished under an increasingly embattled ruling Queen and died out with the last of the Elizabethan courtiers?

The Chivalric Revival appeared early in Elizabeth's reign and may have lasted a half century, perhaps peaking at the 1586 death of that embodiment of chivalry, Sir Philip Sidney, and waning with the 1612 death of another 'gentle knight', Henry, Prince of Wales. The style finally ended with the reign of Charles I, when a more headstrong monarch favoured the sort of radical changes projected by Archbishop Laud and Inigo Jones. Much of the work, of course, was a refurbishment of existing medieval structures, such as Kenilworth Castle, where in 1575 the favourite, Robert Dudley, Earl of Leicester, entertained the queen with the kind of chivalric pageantry typical of the Valois and Hapsburg courts (see Figure 6.5). Kenilworth may have inspired the later Gothic Revival of Sir Walter Scott's romantic fancies, but the ruined works of both John of Gaunt and Robert Dudley can speak of earlier needs and ideals. In his treatments of the 'archaeologies of authorities' and elite residences 'from Medieval to Renaissance', Matthew Johnson offered a spatial analysis of this castle, among others, and determined that its medieval elements and ideologies had been transformed by new work resonating both Elizabethan self-fashioning and contemporary drama.[18] Some scholars have seen particular trends within the Chivalric Revival. Timothy Mowl distinguished between a naturally evolving late, late Gothic style that appears in the

Figure 6.5 Castellated gatehouse built *ca.* 1575 by Robert Dudley at Kenilworth Castle, Warwickshire.

Smythson castle-houses in the north Midlands, and a foppish sort of 'play-castle', found in the south of England.[19] Others have stressed the castle buildings' stylistic heterogeneity.[20]

Leicester's work is in ruins, but not so that of another royal favourite, Sir Walter Raleigh, who on the grounds of the antiquated Sherborne Castle in Dorset erected a castellated lodge with polygonal corner towers. More impressive constructions would take Raleigh's lead. Wardour Castle, Wiltshire, has a stern stone face, punctuated by some danger-ously low windows and an interior court or light well that has classical decoration. The main castle entry has quit the Gothic past but seems lost in the Renaissance, with banded (possibly Tuscan) columns that one hopes supported a missing architrave, and somewhere above, a figured niche (see Figure 6.6). A last English example, Lulworth Castle, Dorset, completed in James's reign, is a four-square structure with round corner towers (see Figure 6.7). The arrangement of its rooms, however, owes little

Figure 6.6 Entrance to Old Wardour Castle, Wiltshire, *ca.* 1580.

to the Middle Ages.[21] With the kitchen and its servants placed 'downstairs' with the cellar storage rooms, the 'upstairs' was unified by a central staircase rising over an entrance lobby. Older traditions did survive, in the hall-and-passage format for formal dining, but the arched service doors have classical round opes above (see Figure 6.8). This chivalric style is a

Figure 6.7 Lulworth Castle, Dorset, *ca.* 1608. Photo courtesy of Roger Leech.

Figure 6.8 Great Hall screens passage at Lulworth Castle, Dorset. Photo courtesy of Roger Leech.

pastiche of elements, but it is placed within a setting of formal gardens in a manner reminiscent of the jewellery worn by men and women of the Renaissance.

Neo-feudal structures were most often erected by the new elite, as much motivated by an instinct to copy the physical surroundings of the ancient aristocracy as an expression of Elizabethan chivalry. Newly created Earl of Leicester, Robert Dudley started the fashion by reworking the vast masses of Kenilworth Castle in the 1560s, and near the end of the tradition, in 1612, Charles Cavendish foresaw his family's rise to the peerage by building the smaller but jewel-like Bolsover Castle.[22] With national recognition in Parliament and knighthoods, families like the Raleighs and the Welds expanded hunting lodges into such show-pieces as Sherborne Castle and Lulworth Castle. 'Arcadian retreats such as Lulworth and Bolsover' Colin Platt considered 'the quintessential "castles" of Spenserian chivalry'.[23] The goal for all these structures was an appearance of military strength. Real defensive capabilities were mixed with and were diluted by fanciful castellations. This still robust archi-tecture was not Horace Walpole's precious Gothik of Strawberry Hill, nor the lumbering Baronial style of Sir Walter Scott's devotees.[24] These Elizabethan castles exhibited ubiquitous crenelation, towers of inappro-priate scale or placement, a profusion of chimneys, and large multi-light windows. In highly decorated elements like fireplaces and doorways, the classical and the feudal met and mingled.

Edmund Spenser's writings, especially *The Faerie Queene*, manifest the dominant spirit of the Elizabethan Age: Renaissance style in the service of chivalry, as classical allegories appear as characters in tales of knights errant.[25] Just as Spenser led Elizabethan literature in a chivalric classicism, so the late Elizabethan architecture of superficial castellation is appropri-ately labelled 'Spenserian'. This style also practiced synthesis, combining the post-medieval arrangement of spatial elements (rooms, stairs, windows) with the decorative forms of a feudal castle. Such a 'Chivalric Revival' was essentially a mutated extenuation of late medieval tendencies that led to a post-Perpendicular Gothic, with hood-mouldings for door-ways and transomed windows, prominent string-courses, and paramili-tary elements like crenelation, projecting battlements, and turreting. Well before the end of the sixteenth century, real military structures employed Italian angled bastions; no Spenserian castle has them. Yet the military elements could be serviceable; hence the musket loops and entry pistol-holes that appear where law and order were least present, in Ireland and Scotland. The presence of hand guns but the absence of cannon, the single armament by which a well-manned castle could be taken or defended, reveals that these structures lacked real military importance.

It was already too late. In the sixteenth century no true castle had risen in England; the state was building forts, and the elite erected fortified houses where needed. In contrast to the bloody religious and dynastic struggles on the Continent, generations of English people knew war as brief overseas expeditions or adventurous naval operations. Perhaps the romance of the military had grown during that time, without the check insured by a stream of casualties, ruined careers, crippling tax burdens, and the bitterness of defeat. It would be ironic if the often insularly minded policies of the Tudors and the fifty years under female monarchs indirectly inspired an architectural style evoking martial prowess. Spenserian architecture flourished at a time when the distinction between fort and fortified house was not yet complete. The homes of the elite reflected the gentility of the knightly class, one part of the medieval world that the sixteenth century refused to reject, but honoured in new forms.

A contemporary treatise reveals what the English really thought about upper class domestic architecture. Barnaby Googe's 1577 'Englished' edition of the German Heresbach's *Foure Bookes of Husbandry* has been discussed in the previous chapter; but in 1613 Gervase Markham published *The English Husbandman* to advise the plain country man, rather than 'instruct gentlemen of dignity who in Architecture are able wonderfully to controle me'.[26] Markham's architectural model for the country house is therefore basic: an H-shape plan usable for all elements of rural society and constructed of stud and plaster, lime and stone, or even of 'courser [sic] woode, and covered with lime and haire'. Nevertheless, the landowner could raise its status by embellishments. 'The foure inward corners of the hall would be convenient for foure turrets', and one could also add bay windows, battlements, and enclose the formal court with a 'tarrisse, or a gatehouse'.[27] For Markham, these details provided the castle-like appearance that 'men of dignity' would naturally respect.

Elizabethan houses in Ireland

What architecture, then, passed from England to Ireland, and was erected by men of money and interest in new buildings? The builders would be those Anglicized and Anglo-Irish families that managed to avoid the deep suspicions of the Tudor dynasty, and the English soldiers, clerks, and even poets 'of fortune' who sought to make names for themselves in the island, often as colonizers. After initial experiments miscarried in both north and south, Elizabethan colonization centred on the province of Munster, whereas renewed colonizing under James took place later in Ulster. Did colonial architecture duplicate that of the homeland, and if so, did it take one style over others?

Irish secular society in the sixteenth century had remained essentially medieval. At its base, peasants lived in round-cornered cabins of stone and thatch. At the extreme upper end, large, heavily guarded castles served as dynastic centres for territorial magnates. The merchant class built urban houses, which ranged from compounds at Kilkenny, to single, street-side structures at Kilmallock.

The Irish elite, both rural and urban, had for some centuries lived in stone tower-houses. Towns are often under-represented in studies of Irish architecture, yet, as the mid-sixteenth-century map of Carrickfergus in Ulster reveals with such clarity, tower-houses dominated the urban landscape.[28] Modern Carrickfergus has lost its tower-houses, but examples can be found from Ardglass, Co. Down, to Youghal, Co. Cork. The visitor to Galway will still see tall urban houses displaying haphazard Italianate decorations that reflect its sea trade connections (Columbus is thought to have visited). The question of halls accompanying urban tower-houses is as yet unanswered, although one may assume that the lower nobility would have used halls as a matter of course on rural sites. By the late sixteenth century an exterior Great Hall may have been used only when larger-than-usual numbers of visitors needed to be entertained. Such guests may have been retainers or allies of lords whose power and stature had grown, but who had not yet expanded their tower-houses. Notable examples of enlarged tower-houses are Blarney, a substantial tower-house later more than doubled in size, and Barryscourt, where the tower-house was sufficiently enlarged to contain large public rooms.[29] Barryscourt also has the remains of an exterior hall, built typically into the bawn wall, and one could argue that the expansion of the tower-house in fact came to replace the exterior hall.

The explorer, colonizer, and courtier, Sir Walter Raleigh, appears again as a builder of note. He was lord of a huge 'signory' of lands that the Queen had confiscated from Irish rebels. On the south coast, his estates along the Blackwater River were served by its port town of Youghal, which followed the political winds and elected Raleigh its mayor. Beside the dominant town church, St Mary's, he built in the late 1580s a home that likely reused a collegiate building made redundant by the Reformation.[30] Myrtle Grove stands today only slightly altered from Raleigh's structure with steep roof, massive chimneys, and gabled dormers (see Figure 6.9).

Figure 6.9 Myrtle Grove, Youghal, Co. Cork.

Figure 6.10 Dromaneen Castle, Co. Cork.

Another Munster example of this style is Dromaneen, an Elizabethan manor house with end chimneys, a pronounced upper-storey string course, and the remnants of dormers (see Figure 6.10).

Even larger, with wide, multi-light windows, a roof with gables and finials, and on the upper floor a long gallery with elaborate Renaissance fireplaces is the well-known late Tudor residence of the Ormond Castle at Carrick-on-Suir (see Figures 1.6, 6.11). Thomas Butler, Earl of Ormond (d. 1614) erected the Elizabethan structure adjacent to the substantial medieval castle at his family seat, in a construction project that probably started in 1565 and with likely alterations and rebuildings may have continued into the 1590s.[31] The extraordinary wealth and power of the Butler earls of Ormonde, who through the Howards and Boleyns were cousins of the Queen, suggests that this was an exceptional structure, more an expression of personal taste and ambition than a model for Tudor architecture in Ireland. The special relationship between Ormond and the Court in London may explain why this could be the only great manor house in Ireland not related to the influx of English Protestants as administrators, soldiers, and landowners that began late in Elizabeth's reign.

Figure 6.11 East side of Ormond residence, Carrig-on-Suir, Co. Tipperary.

Figure 6.12 Dunluce Castle, Co. Antrm.

Other classical elements can be found in Ireland of the early Plantation Period. Far to the north, the Macdonnells, later elevated by James to earldom of Antrim, acquired tracts of land on the Ulster coast. They took the medieval Dunluce Castle (see Figure 6.12) as their seat, which underwent extensive damage in a 1584 siege. James Macdonnell may be responsible for much new construction there, including, as part of an interior structure, the surviving column bases of a crude little portico more suited to the Mediterranean than the North Atlantic. Probably soon after the start of the new century, this opening was largely blocked by an impressive residence that filled most of the original courtyard. Though cramped by existing walls, the new building had a regular front of large windows carried in multi-storey projecting bays.[32]

Renaissance influence also appears in a group of extraordinary structures: large, symmetrical houses with corner towers, similar to, but more house-like than the oversized tower-houses like Bunratty Castle. Looking backward to the castle and forward to the country house, classical elements mix with the palatial, as in the Bishop of Dublin's Rathfarnham Castle.[33] Even more impressive is Kanturk Castle, Co. Cork, built in the 1590s for the head of the McCarthy clan. The size of his residence as well as its defensive potential led the government to worry about possible rebellion and to order construction halted before the roof was in place. Left as a shell for 400 years, there are machicolation at the top, gun loops at the bottom, and even early elements like Gothic doorways inside (see Figures 4.3, 6.13, 6.14). Its large windows and many fireplaces, however, indicate a post-medieval concern for creature comfort. The regularity of plan and elevation looks to contemporary English models, but the provincial effort to reproduce classical details in the main entranceway reflects the Renaissance in the dimmest light.

More commonplace than the transplanted architectural types are the many fortified houses of substance, usually of two or three storeys. A good example is Durrus Court, out on the Sheepshead peninsula, having a symmetrical U-shaped plan with end chimneys (see Figure 6.15). Where the Tudors may have retained crenelation as a decoration for high status buildings, in defence-conscious Ireland both crenelation and machicolation appear regularly on residences. These were fortified manor houses, not quite castles, but not English manor houses, either. It was not a peculiarity of circumstances in Ireland that led to this difference, but actually one in England, which alone among the northern European countries built undefended country houses in the sixteenth century. To live successfully in Ireland, the English erected defendable residences, like the *ca.*

Figure 6.13 Gunloop at Kanturk Castle, Co. Cork.

1600 Mallow Castle of Sir Thomas Norris, President of Munster province (see Figures 1.7, 6.16). Polygonal towers, crenelation, gun loops through the walls, all speak to a concern for defence alongside the expectation of comfort indicated by the wide rooms and numerous windows. Nevertheless, this hybrid form is in no way a 'play castle', as it was built by a capable colonial administrator from a famous military family.

Figure 6.14 Doorway at Kanturk Castle, Co. Cork.

We have seen examples in Irish houses of 'traditional Tudor' and even some classical elements, but both types are few in number compared with the common fortified houses or castle-houses, which were built well into the seventeenth century. The grim reality of self-defence would seem reason enough to eschew the Elizabethan chivalric style. Yet there may have been times when the certainty of English dominance led to over-confidence. Edmund Spenser's rebuilding of Kilcolman Castle seems to be such an example. In spite of (or perhaps related to) the criticism of inadequacy of royal authority in his *View of the Present State of Ireland*, history tells us that Kilcolman was quickly taken and burned by Tyrone's rebels in 1598, and excavation of the ruins determined that the Tudor construction was considerably weaker than that of the medieval builders. Spenser's castle thus seems to have been more for show than real defence,

Figure 6.15 Durrus Court, Co. Kerry.

certainly appropriate for the setting of Sir Walter Raleigh's visit and his first acquaintance with *The Faerie Queene*.

Spenserian architecture in Ireland

The late Tudor period in Ireland saw, as noted above, the continued erection of tower-houses, as well as a few undefended manor houses. The great magnates such as the Earl of Ormond and Sir Walter Raleigh, possessing numerous castles, could afford to establish at least one home on the Elizabethan model. Other landowners, both Irish and English, generally chose the safety of a tower-house, adding modern conveniences when they could afford them. A lord of a 'signory', Spenser used Kilcolman as his administrative seat, but it was also where Raleigh's 1589 visit led to friendship, poetry reading, and eventually Spenser's own trip to London to receive the queen's patronage. It must have appeared appropriate for such a moment, or the meeting would have taken place elsewhere. And because Kilcolman would have been Spenser's creative setting for writing the poetry of Elizabethan chivalry, this structure should, more than any other, reveal to what extent the Spenserian architectural style penetrated Ireland. Indeed, David Newman Johnson has argued that Spenser found that castles remained a necessity in Ireland, and that the *Faerie Queene*

Figure 6.16 Gunloop at Mallow Castle, Co. Cork.

'caused a sympathetic reaction' of English enthusiasts building 'massive castellated structures' in Spenserian style, beginning with Raleigh's Sherborne Castle of 1594.[34] We must remember, though, that most of the leaders involved in the Munster colonization had seen previous military and diplomatic action not just in Ireland, but also in France and the Low Countries, where chivalric styles and the construction of chateaux had been reinvigorated in the days of Charles V and Francois I.

Kilcolman Castle has left few standing remains, but as we saw in Chapter 5, they have been augmented by archaeology to give some picture of Spenser's life there. First of all, he chose to repair and improve a small, probably decayed tower-house and bawn (keep and bailey) in the mild and pastoral countryside of north County Cork. The medieval tower-house and Great Hall he retained, perhaps with little change. He repaired service buildings in the courtyard, and between the tower-house and hall he inserted a new structure, identified as a parlour, with a wooden floor and a large fireplace. Parlours were for domestic use and meals and for more private entertainment than the great hall. Spenser probably roofed his major buildings with wooden shingles and thatched the sheds and barns. He constructed his plastered stone walls with clay bonding, not mortar. A technique revealed by archaeology at similar sites in Ireland, it might indicate preference by the settlers for building upper walls and storeys in timber framing, for which there is no clear evidence as yet.[35] Alternatively, we are reminded by Maurice Howard of how much the Tudors valued appearances over architectural substance in their public buildings and in courtiers' houses, so this may have also applied to Elizabethan Ireland.[36]

At Kilcolman and contemporary castles, one finds an upgrading of the facilities, but there was little room for redesigning interior spaces, and external changes would defeat the purpose of the tower-house as a defensive structure. Filling this need was a new development in Ireland, the defended manor house, which appeared around the last decade of the sixteenth century and continued into the middle of the next century. The fortified manor replaced the tower-house as the typical residence of the landowning elite. Varying greatly in size and scale, these country houses incorporated changes that appeared in new English houses. Some may have been simple extensions of the hall, parlour, entranceway, and staircase plan. Other structures may have been designed to create an internal symmetry of rooms, or to enforce upon the internal space a design determined by external symmetry. Several decorative styles also appear, e.g., the prestigious mantelpieces propagating Renaissance motifs.

New architectural details replaced medieval ones. Hood molding was retained over windows, but less often over doors. Windows were now usually of several lights, and stood vertical rather than horizontal. Also the heights of storeys became uniform. Halls shrank as floors were inserted, making large windows or clerestory illumination redundant. On the other hand, the height of other rooms was increased from the medieval standard, improving living conditions by providing more ventilation and light. All this extra space displayed the new elite's wealth and taste. The emphasis on horizontality also appeared on the external elevation as string courses, which expressed a new sense of proportion and unity of structure. Rising above the roof line were tall, often clustered, chimneys stacks. The roofs were typically crenelated and multi-gabled. Defended manors had gun loops in the walls and pistol holes at the entrances, while projecting machicolations were carried over from the tower-house.

Chapter 4 examined several types of plan common to Irish fortified country houses, which point to a development of defended residences from tower-house to manor house.[37] Perhaps the earliest identifiable X-plan is the Archbishop of Dublin's country seat at Rathfarnham, but better known is the McCarthys' huge rectangular mansion with projecting corner towers, Kanturk Castle, which has stood unroofed and unfloored since the end of Elizabeth's reign. Many houses took a Y shape. Rudimentary wings and an opposite stair tower appear at the well-fortified Mallow Castle built by the President of Munster, Sir Thomas Norris, about 1600. A much larger and more developed Y-plan is Coppinger's Court, erected early in Charles's reign. The Z-plan house is most prevalent in Northern Ireland, a likely influence from the Scottish tradition of Z-shaped tower-house castles.[38] At the Ulster bawn settlements established in the Jacobean 'plantations', many defended houses had projecting towers at two opposite corners. This simple arrangement was a serious military feature, in that it provided flanking fire along all sides of the building.

Spenserian style and the architecture of empire

Our original question was whether a relationship existed between the continued tradition of defended residences in Ireland and the English 'chivalric revival' in architecture. To answer this, we need to address several specific points. First, to what degree were the Irish domestic fortifications practical? We can note some common elements: gun loops, restricted entrances (usually two), towers, crenelation and machicolation, but no moats. These measures seem designed to protect as well as

impress. Second, how does the Irish experience relate to the developments in rural residences of the English elite like Spenser and Raleigh?
Apparently very little. While keep-towers and gate-towers played an
important role in fifteenth-century English construction, this waned in
the sixteenth century, as society favoured the Tudor country house. It
was the opposite in Ireland, where few manor houses were built. Tower-
houses, the domestic residences of the Irish elite in the fifteenth and
sixteenth centuries, were supplanted by Elizabethan and Jacobean fortified houses. Beyond the ubiquitous Renaissance fireplaces, classical details
were usually applied idiosyncratically, like the doorway at Kanturk and
the portico at Dunluce. Early seventeenth-century Ireland even witnessed
a possible attempt at a Palladian-style building in the unfinished vice-
royal palace at Jigginstown (see Figure 1.8). Charles's governor, the Earl
of Strafford, sought to express absolutist power through a new style and a
gargantuan scale, but the project ended with the earl's beheading in 1639.

It would be unwise to consider the late tower-houses and fortified houses of Ireland as Spenserian-style mock castles. True, these
defended homes were not castles in the traditional, medieval sense, but
they were expected to deter a limited threat. For example, the gun loops
in domestic fortified houses are clearly not decorative, and are just as
functional as those found at Fort Mountjoy in Ulster, which was built as
field headquarters for Charles Blount, Lord Mountjoy, Elizabeth's victo-
rious commander (see Figure 2.11). The defensive elements of fortified
houses were real, not symbols of chivalry. Architecture after 1598 shows
that the English colonial elite came to employ the idiom of force and
largely rejected traditional Irish forms like the tower-house, which had
been favoured by Edmund Spenser and others who fled or died in the
uprising.

With a better understanding of the architecture of colonial Ireland, we
must now consider to what degree it was relevant to the broader context of
English expansion, to a nascent British Empire. We have been examining
works from the 1580s to the 1620s, essentially a forty-year generation
of both English colonizers and the Irish who associated with them. The
architectural examples are admittedly a small selection. Yet the focus in
this chapter has not been on the commonplace of vernacular architecture,
but on the buildings of the elite – of the Great, in reinterpretation of the
Tudor–Stuart 'Great Rebuilding'. The grandest of residences would always
have been few in number, though naturally their numbers increased over
the generations. The great majority of the substantial houses erected in
Ireland under Elizabeth and James belong to one architectural type, the

defended manor house. Yet finding elements of all three domestic Elizabethan architectural types – traditional Tudor, classical, and chivalric –
also suggests that, for some members of the elite, their houses represent
something other than the fruits of colonization, or colonialism in its basic
sense, and that is the idea of empire.[39]

A colony is a dependent territory economically developed to serve the
home country, whilst an imperial province is equal to other provinces and
has a certain 'share' in the empire, whether Roman, Carolingian, or Napo-
leonic. This community of ethnicities or states is the strength and basis of
empires. Writing in the twentieth century, an Irish scholar looked back
on the post-Cromwell, late seventeenth century as a time when 'English
families in Ireland looked upon England as unquestionably their mother
country, and Englishmen in Ireland regarded it as a place in which they
could get a political job or make money in a commercial enterprise, as
until recently they have looked upon South Africa or Jamaica'.[40] In early
modern Ireland, especially in the Elizabethan period, those who identified themselves as colonists saw themselves as planting settlements in a
primitive, alien, and dangerous land, and took measures to defend themselves. Others, whether idealistic or naive, may have occupied medieval
structures to substantiate their claims, but typically built according to
English non-defensive fashions and conventions, seeing Englishness in
Ireland, where there was only promise and potential. For them, an imperial mentality, not a colonial outlook, determined their choice of building.
Edmund Spenser himself saw fit to proclaim the existence, and extent,
of the Elizabethan Empire. A. L. Rowse noted how Spenser picked up
Raleigh's theme of imperialism when he dedicated *The Faerie Queene*:
'To the most high mightie and magnificant Empress renowned for pietie
vertue and all gratious government Elizabeth by the grace of God Queene
of England Fraunce and Ireland and of Virginia'.[41]

Spenserian chivalric architecture in England was adopted by those of
the Tudor elite, like Raleigh, who followed the tradition of the nobles
of the Sword and spurned the mixed Renaissance style employed by
Burleigh and other nobility of the Robe. In Ireland, Elizabethan colonization saw old tower-house castles refitted and reused by landowners like
Spenser, whilst a few members of the elite erected undefended manor
houses. But Spenser's castle was apparently not really strengthened at all.
It and nearly every other Munster castle held by English landowners in
October 1598 were taken by Irish rebels and destroyed. One must assume
that Spenser's own residence was in style and intent Spenserian, a castle,
in Ben Jonson's words, 'built with ayre'.

Elizabethan and Jacobean architecture in Ireland therefore conveyed a dual message. First, the initial colonists' reuse of medieval castles identified them as a knightly class and their estates as a continuity of the feudal basis of land tenure from the Anglo-Norman conquest. Second, their failure to suppress the Irish brought into power after 1598 other English who claimed no feudal heritage but saw themselves as reformed and modernized, and their houses as seats of power and wealth. They spurned the old castles for new houses that would be fortified – unsuitable against a real army, but adequate protection against the sudden raid of a few dozen ruffians. Facing no proper military opponent after the Nine Years War, the new English expected to rule a naturally wicked population of rebels, traitors, and the uncivilized 'wild' Irish. Spenserian architecture in England and Ireland had been the choice of Elizabethans who saw themselves as equals to the lords of the past. The newer fortified houses were built by seventeenth-century men who distrusted honor and loyalty. What faith they had was put in money and muskets, and therein lay the fate of Ireland for the next five centuries.

Notes

1 J. H. Harris (ed.), *Eastward Ho, by Chapman, Jonson, and Marston*. Yale Studies in English 73 (New Haven and London, 1926), p. 27 (lines 762–3). The *Oxford Dictionary of Quotations* (2nd edn, 1955) p. 280, ascribes the authorship to Jonson alone.

2 D. Crossley, *Post-Medieval Archaeology in Britain* (Leicester, 1990), pp. 107–13.

3 W. Maley, *Salvaging Spenser: Colonialism, Culture and Identity* (London, 1997), devotes a chapter to Spenser's 'planting a new culture beyond the Pale', pp. 48–77, viewing him as a spokesman for a colonial imperative and a pragmatic participant in the Munster Plantation.

4 A full review of the topic is found in M .W. Barley 'Rural housing in England', in J. Thirsk (ed.), *The Agrarian History of England and Wales Vol. IV 1500-1640* (Cambridge, 1967), pp. 696–766; 'Formality began to be imposed in the Elizabethan age and later, under the influence of Renaissance ideas to which social needs were subordinate', p. 698.

5 For a discussion of this term, see M. Howard, 'Self-fashioning and the classical moment in mid-sixteenth-century English architecture' in L. Gent and N. Llewellyn (eds) *Renaissance Bodies: The Human Figure in English Culture c.1540–1660* (London, 1990), pp. 198–217. Perhaps the courtier class gained a certain independence of mind – and taste – away from the monarch during the less effective reigns of Henry VIII's children.

6 See N. Davis (ed.), *The Paston Letters* (Oxford and New York, 1983; orig. pub. 1963).

7 These buildings are reviewed in M. W. Thompson, *The Decline of the Castle* (Cambridge, 1987), pp. 87–96, 99–100.

8 W. G. Hoskins, 'The rebuilding of rural England, 1560–1640', *Past and Present* 4 (1953), pp. 44–59.

9 M. H. Johnson,'Rethinking the Great Rebuilding', *Oxford J. Archaeol.* 12 (1993), pp. 117–24.

10 M. Howard, 'Self-fashioning and the classical moment in mid-sixteenth-century English architecture', in. L. Gent and N. Llewellyn (eds), *Renaissance Bodies*, pp. 198–217; and 'Civic buildings and courtier houses: new techniques and materials for architectural

ornament', in D. Gaimster and P. Stamper (eds), *The Age of Transition: The Archaeology of English Culture 1400–1600* (Oxford, 1997), pp. 105–13.

11 M. Girouard, *Robert Smythson and the Architecture of the Elizabethan Era* (South Brunswick, NJ, 1967); M. Airs, *The Making of the English Country House 1500–1640* (London, 1975); and N. Cooper, 'The gentry house in the Age of Transition', in Gaimster and Stamper (eds), *The Age of Transition*, pp. 115–26.

12 For the traditional style, see S. E. Castle, *Domestic Gothic of the Tudor Period* (Jamestown, NY, 1927); Nikolaus Pevsner considers it a continuance of the Perpendicular tradition, and English architecture between 1530 and 1620 'a composite phenomena', *An Outline of European Architecture* (Harmondsworth, 1943, 7th edn repr.1982), pp. 304–7.

13 T. Mowl, *Elizabethan and Jacobean Style* (London, 1993), pp. 105–23.

14 See M. Howard, *The Vyne* (London, 1998).

15 A. L. Rowse, *The Elizabethan Experience: The Cultural Achievement* (Chicago, 1972) considers buildings in classical style to be the initiative of an 'Edwardian circle', among whom he numbers Smith, Cecil, Bacon, Thyyne, and Heneage, pp. 143–5.

16 M. Girouard, *Robert Smythson and the Architecture of the Elizabethan Era* (New York, 1990) offers a thorough treatment of what are essentially palaces of magnates. Mowl, *Elizabethan and Jacobean Style*, pp. 106–10, differentiates between a north Midlands continuing tradition (via Smythson) of great houses blending architectural styles in search of a chivalric device and a southern 'play-castle' formula of Gothic revival for noble family holiday homes.

17 Girouard considered the late Elizabethan 'compact house', as the end product of 'a tendency for even large houses to do without courtyards and cohere into a single dominating mass', *Life in the English Country House* (New Haven and London, 1978), pp. 114–18.

18 M. H. Johnson, *The Archaeology of Capitalism* (Oxford, 1996), pp. 122–3; and *Behind the Castle Gate: From Medieval to Renaissance* (London and New York, 2002), pp. 136–60.

19 Mowl, *Elizabethan and Jacobean Style*, p. 108.

20 P. A. Faulkner, *Bolsover Castle* (London, 1972; repub. London, 1985); Girouard, *Robert Smythson*.

21 Girouard, *Robert Smythson*, pp. 88–93.

22 Mowl, *Elizabethan and Jacobean Style*, pp. 71– 81, 113–22, describes the significance of Dudley's new architecture and entertainments as well as the achievement of Cavendish and his builder Smythson.

23 C. Platt, *The Great Rebuildings of Tudor and Stuart England: Revolutions in Architectural Taste* (London, 1994), p. 96.

24 M. W. Thompson, *Decline of the Castle*, pp. 160–1.

25 See D. N. Johnson, 'Kilcolman Castle', in A. C. Hamilton (ed.), *The Spenser Encyclopedia* (Toronto, 1990), pp. 417–22; for Spenserian architecture, p. 422.

26 G. Markham, *The English Husbandman* (London, 1613; repr. New York and London, 1982), pp. A3v-Bv: 'Of the Situation of the Husbandmans house; the necessaries there to belonging, together with the modell thereof', in the inserted 'A Former Part before the first Part [of the] Introduction'.

27 The placement of the turrets over the central section of the house, rather than the wings, may suggest a function as belvederes for watching the hunt. Markham also suggested 'bay windowes ... formed in any curious manner' to raise its status: G. Markham, *The English Husbandman*, p. A3r.

28 British Museum Cotton MS. Augustus I. ii42. Reproduced in P. D. A. Harvey, *Maps in Tudor England* (Chicago and London, 1993), p. 99.

29 H. G. Leask, *Irish Castles and Castellated Houses* (Dundalk, 1941; repr. 1986), pp. 113–16.

30 G. H. Orpen, 'Raleigh's House, Youghal', *J. Royal Society of Antiquaries of Ireland* (1903),

pp. 310–12. Recent observations on the building's architectural history can be found in Tadhg O'Keeffe, 'Plantation-era great houses in Munster: a note on Sir Walter Raleigh's house and its context', pp. 274–89 in T. Herron and M. Potterton (eds) *Ireland in the Renaissance* c. *1540-1660* (Dublin, 2007).

31 The dating is largely based on chimney plasterwork date of 1565 and comparison of the structure's extensive surviving plasterwork to contemporay examples and publications. See Jane Fenlon, *Ormond Castle* (Dublin, 1996) and 'The decorative plasterwork at Ormond Castle – a unique survival', *Architectural Hist.* 41 (1998), pp 67–81; and Hanneke Ronnes, 'Continental traces at Carrick-on-Suir and contemporary Irish castle: a preliminary study of date-and-initial stones', pp. 255–73 in T. Herron and M. Potterton (eds) *Ireland in the Renaissance ca. 1540-1660* (Dublin, 2007). But see also D. M. Waterman, 'Some Irish seventeenth-century houses and their architectural ancestry', in M. Jope (ed.), *Studies in Building History. Essays dedicated to B. H. St J. O'Neil* (London, 1961), pp. 251–74, see p. 252; M. Craig, *The Architecture of Ireland from the Earliest Times to 1880* (Dublin and London, 1982), pp. 113–14; Leask, *Irish Castles*, p. 98. Leask (pp. 146–7), attributes Carrick to 'the last years of Elizabeth's reign or early in that of her successor', presumably *ca.* 1590 to *ca.* 1610, because its wide windows with rounded heads and its rounded head doorway make it 'practically contemporary [with] Kanturk and Mallow.'

32 See the guide by H. Dixon, *Dunluce Castle, County Antrim* (Belfast, 1985).

33 Craig, *Architecture of Ireland*, pp. 114–22.

34 Johnson, 'Kilcolman Castle', p. 422.

35 For examples later than the Munster colonization, see M. Ponsford, 'Post-Medieval Britain and Ireland in 1990', *Medieval Archaeol.* 25 (1991), pp. 115–70, pp. 142–3 for a note on two clay-bonded walled late seventeenth-century buildings in Limerick; and C. Manning, 'A Sheila-na-Gig from Glanworth Castle, Co. Cork', in E. Rynne and H. M. Roe (eds), *Figures from the Past* (Dun Loaghaire, 1987), pp. 278–82, and *Clough Outer: A Midlands Castle in Co. Cavan* (Bray, 1999).

36 See M. Howard, 'Civic buildings and courtier houses: new techniques and materials for architectural ornament', in Gaimster and Stamper (eds), *The Age of Transition*, pp. 104–13.

37 E. Klingelhofer, 'Vernacular architecture of the Munster Plantation', paper presented to the American Historical Association, 1996. Plans of Tudor-Stuart houses, though not following the XYZ typology, are illustrated in N. McCullough and V. Mulvin, *A Lost Tradition: The Nature of Architecture in Ireland* (Dublin, 1987, repr. 1989), pp. 43–55. For earlier ideas on the subject, see Waterman, 'Some Irish seventeenth-century houses'.

38 P. M. Kerrigan, *Castles and Fortifications in Ireland 1485-1945* (Cork, 1995), pp. 68–72, notes several examples of the T-plan manor house within Ulster plantation bawns.

39 It must be admitted that David Quinn expressed doubts about when and how Ireland was a colony: 'Irish history in the sixteenth century is not merely and solely that of the struggle of the English crown to master a rebellious fief, nor is it wholly that of the domination of a native population by a wave of conquering English. It is, at certain times and places, mainly the one, or mainly the other. A simple and direct contrast between Ireland and the greatest of the sixteenth century colonies, the Spanish empire in America, is not, therefore, possible.' See 'Ireland and sixteenth century European expansion', in T. D. Williams (ed.), *Historical Studies* 1 (London, 1958), pp. 22–32, quote from pp. 22–3. The Munster Plantation was one of those times and places, but even then and there, it was a piecemeal colony involving only one quarter of the land.

40 E. MacLysaght, *Irish Life in the Seventeenth Century* (Dublin, 1939, repr. 1979), pp. 34–5.

41 E. Spenser, 'The Faerie Queene', p. 2 in F. M. Padelford (ed.), *The Works of Edmund Spenser; The Faerie Queene: Book One* (Baltimore, 1932). A. L. Rowse, *The Elizabethan Age: The Cultural Achievement* (Chicago, 1972), pp. 56–7, p. 179. But Spenser's 'colonialism' has been the subject of much lively debate; see Maley, *Salvaging Spenser*.

7

Conclusions

Had I plantation of this isle, my lord,– ...
And were the king on't, what would I do?...
All things in common nature would produce
Without sweat or endeavour: treason, felony,
Sword, pike, knife, gun, or need of any engine,
Would I not have: but nature should bring forth,
Of its own kind, all foison, all abundance,
To feed my innocent people.

William Shakespeare, *The Tempest*, 1611

Proto-colonial archaeology of Elizabethan Ireland, particularly in the Irish Republic, has only recently begun, and caution warns against advancing firm conclusions at this stage. Nevertheless, some general observations are justified concerning the twelve-year Elizabethan colonial settlement, or 'planting', of Munster, because even limited fieldwork can significantly correct research all too dependent upon insufficient documentation. Elizabethan Ireland was certainly not the 'brave new world' that Shakespeare posited in *The Tempest*, but it may be that he had in mind just those problems incurred by the plantation of Munster.

Munster colonial villages, large and small, attempted to replicate what existed in England: individual house plots, each probably with a small garden or orchard attached, fronted streets and greens at regular intervals. Families lived in half-timber houses with upper floors, similar to those they had left in England, warmed themselves by a wall-side fireplace instead of a central hearth, and attended services in refurbished medieval churches reserved for the Anglican Church of Ireland, Catholic public worship having been officially banned. Settlers were attracted to Munster because of the availability of land. Allotted fields and pastures adequately supported their households in a mixed farming regime that exported dairy products, wool, and hides. Some settlers would have been involved in the highly profitable timber industry (which sold barrel staves to Spain) and attempts at iron working. Archaeology demonstrates their trade with the West Country ports, bringing them English goods like the serviceable Devonshire pottery as well as items from the Continent like Iberian oil jars or Rhenish beer jugs. Outside the villages, in the shadow of the great woods, native Irish still lived in traditional hamlets, often providing the workforce for farm and forest.

Munster may very well have seen as strong a division between the classes as existed in Tudor England. Data is now insufficient to reconstruct settlers' living conditions, but the excavated evidence does suggest that whilst the colonial elite had a far richer, varied diet than the typical native household, in some ways it was not dissimilar to that of townsfolk in Limerick or Cork. Colonial settlers remain enigmatic, but the architectural record reveals the scale of difference between castle and cottage. The granting of land in 1200-acre 'signories' was a feudal arrangement, and these grantees were lords in law and in fact, living in castles and fortified houses that had been already suppressed in England. The leading men and their families may have been estranged nearly as much from their English dependents as they were from the expropriated Irish, and this no doubt contributed to the colony's rapid demise.

The economy of early modern Ireland was significantly different from its late medieval economy. It had become a place of profit for those who held the land as Elizabeth's grantees, and also for those who traded in the port towns. The origins of the Anglo-Irish Ascendancy can be traced to Elizabethan policies, interrupted but also reinforced by the Nine Years War, and to the government's ready acceptance that members of the new colonial administration would find their fortunes in assembling confiscated estates. Not unlike the American Confederacy in 1865, after a bloody civil war Ireland too fell under military occupation, and its landed estates became objects of confiscation for the new political masters. All this Elizabeth, her ministers, and the investors in Ireland could not have foreseen. They had hoped to transform Ireland into an extension of England, with an identical culture based upon the same laws, language, and religion, but also into a place of opportunity for individuals with ambition and friends at Court. The military victory of the dying Elizabeth provided James with the opportunity to create, instead, only a wealthy ruling class. Its domination of the economy closed southern Ireland to investment by joint-stock companies and discouraged broader English settlement there, which benefitted transatlantic colonization.

Figure 7.1 Lisgriffin Castle, Co. Cork, an early seventeenth-century Barry residence.

Both Munster and Ulster had confident developers such as Raleigh, Boyle, and Crooke who tried to establish population centres at strategic locations and to make such settlement profitable and secure by ruthlessly exploiting the natural resources and the native population. Yet there were important differences between the colonies. In Elizabethan Munster, new settlers were always a minority. Until the Irish defeat at Kinsale, Elizabethan 'plantings' were limited spatially and legally. The smaller towns and villages in Munster proved ill-prepared for defence, and the English-owned castles, bawns, and fortified houses of the countryside rarely withstood the rebels. The generation after Kinsale rebuilt most of them, as at Kilcolman, and erected many new fortified houses. And like the castles of the past, they served an elite of both Irish and English descent (see Figure 7.1). Rural fortified domestic sites are common in the Ulster Plantation, and American archaeologists are finding similar, if wooden, structures in seventeenth-century Virginia. The 1993–96 excavations at Edmund Spenser's castle sought to discover to what extent the castle defences had been maintained, improved, or possibly weakened by Spenser's rebuilding of a late medieval Irish tower-house and bawn.

The twelve-year span of the First Plantation of Munster may be too brief to have produced substantive archaeological information on the precise modes of domination and resistance in Elizabethan Ireland. Yet the colonial documents, mostly reports from military and civil officers to Elizabeth and her senior counselors, focus on just those issues, which are essentially the reason why the documents were created: to ensure English dominance and to forestall or eliminate resistance. Archaeology can, however, supply details about changing patterns of settlement, as the Irish *clachans* were abandoned in much the same fashion as the later Highland clearances in Scotland. And more light could be shed on the nature of Irish resistance, described by contemporaries in the same terms of treacherous barbarity ascribed to the American Indians. Further study of military sites could produce evidence, independent of English sources, about the level of Irish technological capabilities in the armed struggle that overwhelmed the Elizabethan colony, but would subsequently also end Irish independence.

The next stage of proto-colonial archaeology in southern Ireland will need to advance beyond the excavation of 'type sites' closely tied to the documents and the few surviving maps. In Northern Ireland, a series of plantation maps by Thomas Craven in the 1620s and 1630s offers many details of both colonial and native landscapes; these will continue to be an important asset for proto-colonial research.[1] Eventually, data will be accumulated throughout Ireland to examine the deeper, more difficult questions about social and economic forces prevailing at the local level and, most problematic of all, the relations between the Elizabethan settlers and the Irish whom they displaced, but did not destroy.[2] Important work is already being undertaken in the urban centres, where a much-needed chronology of artifact types (of which the most important are the regional potteries) has been initiated from excavations in Waterford and Cork, as well as Dublin – medieval walled enclosures that were not part of Tudor and Stuart colonizing efforts.

A 'critical mass' of physical evidence is needed to identify the material cultures of the three groups competing in the proto-colonial period: the native Irish, the 'Old English' of Catholic and Norman heritage, and the 'New English' Protestant colonists. At that point, research will come up against serious methodological questions. How do patterns of artifact assemblages explain the socioeconomic conditions determining lives? If ethnic differences can be established, how do they inform us of relations among the three groups? Answers to both questions could be complicated by the effects on material culture of a fourth group of people whose behaviour was characterized by political pragmatism and about whom we know very little from colonial documents: the merchants and artisans of the old medieval cities, whose fluctuating loyalties are likely to reflect ambiguities of identity. The simplest approach would be to look for temporal changes from one material culture type to another, and ascertain the chronology and nature (e.g. destructiveness) of such changes. Then more discrete questions can be addressed. What exactly was the make-up of the tenant population in Elizabethan Munster? Where were English colonists the majority, and where did the native Irish dominate? Is this reflected in the later histories of these localities? Can one estimate cost/resource factors, especially those of food and shelter? In certain circumstances, rubbish pits, privies, and middens can offer biological evidence for the quantity and variety of diet. Colonial standards of living could be addressed by a study of pottery containers, their volume, strength, and distance of travel, but are these data relevant for the largely aceramic Irish peasantry? Materials and labour could be compared for building types, on a site-by-site basis, but can these be applied more broadly: spatially, for example, regionally in terms of the prevalence of building types, and temporally, in terms of durability or replacement rate?

The discrete questions posed at this secondary level of investigation will prove difficult to answer, but they are, after all, the ones worth asking. They point us to the final level of investigation, explaining the behaviour of identifiable groups and their members, in specific historical circumstances. Changes in the intellectual and political climates – north and south of the Irish border – are bringing opportunities to seek out archaeological evidence relating to the trauma that has deeply affected both Irish and English, both Protestant and Catholic, and that still scars many. Let us trust that the ghost of the colonial past can be exorcized, and that the careful assemblage of facts will challenge and dispel the myths of both conquered and conqueror. Archaeology, starting with Elizabethan castles and colonists, may at last offer the means to clarify Edmund Spenser's contradictory Irelands: 'Faerie Land' and 'wretched Realme'.

Notes

1 J. H. Andrews, *Irish Maps* (Dublin, 1978), pp. 11–13.
2 See D. B. Quinn, *The Elizabethans and the Irish* (Ithaca, NY, 1966).

Select bibliography

Airs, M. (1975) *The Making of the English Country House 1500–1640*, London.

Andrews, K. R., N. P. Canny, and P. E. H. Hair (1979), *The Westward Enterprise: English Activities in Ireland, the Atlantic, and America 1480–1650*, Detroit and Liverpool.

Barley, M. W. (1967) 'Rural housing in England', pp. 696–766 in J. Thirsk, *The Agrarian History of England and Wales Vol. IV 1500–1640*, Cambridge.

Barnby, H. (1969) 'The sack of Baltimore', *J. Cork Hist. and Archaeol. Soc.* 74, pp. 106–7.

Barry, T. B. (1987) *The Archaeology of Medieval Ireland*, London and New York.

—— (2000) *A History of Settlement in Ireland*, London and New York.

Bartlett, W. H. (1842) *Scenery and Antiquities of Ireland*, London.

Beresford, M. (1967) *New Towns of the Middle Ages: Town Plantation in England, Wales and Gascony*, London.

Blades, B. S. (1981) '"In the manner of England": tenant housing in the Londonderry Plantation', *Ulster Folklife* 27, pp. 39–56.

—— (1986) 'English villages in the Londonderry Plantation', *Post-Medieval Archaeol.* 20, pp. 257–69.

Brunskill, R. W. (1971) *Illustrated Handbook of Vernacular Architecture*, London.

Buchanan, R. H. (1986) 'Towns and plantations', pp. 85–98 in W. Nolan, *The Shaping of Ireland: The Geographic Perspective*, Dublin.

Butlin, R. A. (1976) 'The land and the people', pp. 141–86 in T. W. Moody *et al.*, *Modern Ireland 1534–1691*, vol. 3, *A New History of Ireland*, Oxford.

Canny, N. (1976) *The Elizabethan Conquest of Ireland: A Pattern Established 1567–76*, Hassocks, Sussex; New York, 1977.

—— (1989) 'Introduction: Spenser and the reform of Ireland', pp. 9–24 in P. Coughlan, *Spenser in Ireland: An Interdisciplinary Perspective*, Cork

—— (1998) *The Origins of Empire: British Overseas Enterprise to the Close of the Seventeenth Century*, vol. 1, Oxford History of the British Empire, Oxford, New York.

Castle, S. E. (1927) *Domestic Gothic of the Tudor Period*, Jamestown, NY.

Cecil, Lord David (1984) *Hatfield House*, London.

Cheney, E. P. (1907) 'Some English conditions surrounding the settlement of Virginia', *American Hist. Rev.* 12, pp. 509–28.

Coombes, J. (1972) 'The sack of Baltimore: a forewarning', *J. Cork Hist. and Archaeol. Soc.* 77, pp. 60–1.

Cooper, N. (1997) 'The gentry house in the Age of Transition', in D. Gaimster and P. Stamper, *The Age of Transition: The Archaeology of English Culture 1400–1600*, Oxford.

Craig, M. (1982) *The Architecture of Ireland from the Earliest Times to 1880*, Dublin.

Crossley, D. (1990) *Post-Medieval Archaeology in Britain*, Leicester.

Cruickshank, C. G. (1966) *Elizabeth's Army*, Oxford, 1st edn, 1946.

Dee, J. (1577) *The Perfecte Arte of Navigation*, London; repr. Amsterdam, New York, 1968.

Dixon, H. (1985) *Dunluce Castle*, County Antrim, Belfast.

Dixon, P. and B. Lot (1993) 'The courtyard and the tower: contexts and symbols in the development of late medieval great houses', *J. British Archaeol. Assoc.* 146, pp. 93–101.

Dunlop, R. (1888) 'The Plantation of Munster, 1584–1589', *English Hist. Rev.* 3, pp. 250–69.

—— (1891) 'The Plantation of Leix and Offaly', *English Hist. Rev.* 6, pp. 61–96.

—— (1924) 'An unpublished survey of the Plantation of Munster in 1622', *J. Royal Soc. Antiquaries of Ireland* 54, pp. 128–46.

Ellis, Steven G. (1985) *Tudor Ireland: Crown, Community and the Conflict of Cultures. 1470–1603*, London and New York.

Falls, C. (1970) *Elizabeth's Irish Wars*, New York and London, 1950.

Falkiner, C. L. (1904) *Illustrations of Irish History, Mainly of the Seventeenth Century*, London.

Faulkner, P. A. (1972) *Bolsover Castle*, London; repr. 1985.

Fenlon, J. (1996) *Ormond Castle*, Dublin.

—(1998) 'The decorative plasterwork at Ormond Castle – a unique survival', *Architectural Hist.* 41, pp. 67–81.

Foster, R. F. (1988) *Modern Ireland 1600–1972*, New York.

Gillespie, R. (1991) *The Transformation of the Irish Economy 1550–1700*, Studies in Irish Economic and Social History, Dundalgan.

Girouard, M. (1967) *Robert Smythson and the Architecture of the Elizabethan Era*, South Brunswick, NJ, repr. 1990.

—— (1978) *Life in the English Country House: A Social and Architectural History*, New Haven and London.

Gottfried, R. (1946) *Spenser's Prose Works*, Baltimore.

Googe, Barnaby (1577) *Foure Bookes of Husbandry, collected by M. Conradus Heresbachus.... Newely Englished, and increased, by Barnabe Googe, Esquire*, London.

Greenlaw, E. *et al.* (eds), *The Works of Edmund Spenser*, Baltimore, 1932, repr. 1966.

Hadfield, A. (1997) *Edmund Spenser's Irish Experience: Wilde Fruit and Salvage Soyl*, Oxford.

Hale, J. R. (1982) 'The defense of the realm, 1485–1558', pp. 367–401, in H. M. Colvin, *History of the King's Works Vol. IV 1485–1660 (Part II)*, London.

—— (1983) *Renaissance War Studies*, London.

—— (1985) *War and Society in Renaissance Europe 1520–1620*, London.

Harvey, P. D. A. (1993a) *Maps in Tudor England*, Chicago and London.

—— (1993b) 'Estate surveyors and the spread of the scale-map in England 1550–80', *Landscape Hist.* 15, pp. 37–49.

Hayes-McCoy, G. A. (1964) *Ulster and other Irish Maps c. 1600*, Dublin.

—— (1969) *Irish Battles*, London.

Healy, J. N. (1988) *The Castles of County Cork*, Cork.

Henley, P. (1928) *Spenser in Ireland*, Cork and London.

Hinton, E. M. (1935) *Ireland Through Tudor Eyes*, Philadelphia.

Hoskins, W.G. (1953) 'The rebuilding of rural England, 1560–1640', *Past and Present* 4, pp. 44–59.

Howard, M. (1990) 'Self-fashioning and the classical moment in mid-sixteenth-century architecture', pp. 198–217 in L. Gent and N. Llewellyn *Renaissance Bodies: The Human Figure in English Culture c.1540–1660*, London.

—— (1997) 'Civic buildings and courtier houses: new techniques and materials for architectural ornament', pp. 105–13 in D. Gaimster and P. Stamper, *The Age of Transition: The Archaeology of English Culture 1400–1600*, Oxford.

—— (1998) *The Vyne*, London.

Hunter, J. R. (1971) 'Towns in the Ulster Plantation', *Studia Hibernica* 11, pp. 40–79.

Johnson, D. N. (1990) 'Kilcolman Castle', pp. 417–22 in A. C. Hamilton, *The Spenser Encyclopedia*, Toronto.

—— (1992) 'Later medieval castles' pp. 188–92 in M. Ryan, *The Illustrated Archaeology of Ireland*, Dublin.

Johnson, M. H. (1993) 'Rethinking the Great Rebuilding', *Oxford J. Archaeol.* 12 No. 1, pp. 117–24.

—— (1996) *The Archaeology of Capitalism*, Oxford.

—— (2002) *Behind the Castle Gate: From Medieval to Renaissance*, London and New York.

Kerrigan, P. (1982) 'Seventeenth century fortifications, forts and garrisons in Ireland: a preliminary list', *The Irish Sword* 14 Nos 54, 55 (1980–82), pp. 3–24, 135–56.

—— (1995) *Castles and Fortifications in Ireland 1485–1945*, Cork.

Klingelhofer, E. (1992) 'The Renaissance fortifications at Dunboy Castle, 1602: a report on the 1989 excavations', *J. Cork Hist. and Archaeol. Soc.* 97, pp. 85–96.

—— (1997) '*Castles Built with Air*: Spenserian architecture in Ireland', pp. 149–54 in G. de Boe and F. Verhaeghe, *Military Studies in Medieval Europe*, Papers of the 'Medieval Europe Brugge 1997' Conference, vol. 11, Instituut voor het Archeologisch Patrimonium Zellik, Belgium.

—— (1999a) 'Proto-colonial archaeology: the case of Elizabethan Ireland', pp. 164–79 in P. Funari, M. Hall, and S. Jones, *Back from the Edge: Archaeology in History*, London.

—— (1999b) 'The castle of the *Faerie Queene*, probing the ruins of Edmund Spenser's Irish home', *Archaeology*, March/April, pp. 48–52.

—— (1999c) 'Elizabethan settlements at Mogeely Castle, Curraglass and Carrigeen, Co. Cork (Part I)', *J. Cork Hist. and Archaeol.Soc.*, 104, pp. 97–110 .

—— (2000) 'Elizabethan settlements at Mogeely Castle, Curraglass and Carrigeen, Co. Cork Part II', *J. Cork Hist. and Archaeol. Soc.*, 105, pp. 155–74.

—— (2003) 'The architecture of empire: Elizabethan country houses in Ireland', pp. 102–15 in S. Lawrence, *The Archaeology of the British*, London.

—— (2005) 'Edmund Spenser at Kilcolman Castle: the archaeological evidence', *Post-Medieval Archaeol.* 39:1, pp. 133–54.

Lacy, B. (1991) 'The archaeology of the Ulster Plantation', pp. 201–5 in M. Ryan, *The Illustrated Archaeology of Ireland*, Dublin.

Leask, H. G. (1941) *Irish Castles and Castellated Houses*, Dundalk, repr. 1986.

—— (1944) 'Mallow Castle, Co. Cork', *J. Cork Hist. and Archaeol. Soc.* 49, pp. 19–24.

Lennon, C. (1995) *Sixteenth-Century Ireland: The Incomplete Conquest*, New York.

Loeber, R. (1991) *The Geography and Practice of English Colonization in Ireland*, Irish Settlement Series 3, Athlone.

Loeber, R. and M. Stouthamer-Loeber (1987) 'The lost architecture of the Wexford Plantation', pp. 173–200 in K. Whelan, *Wexford: History and Society. Interdisciplinary Essays on the History of an Irish County*, Dublin.

Loeber, R. and G. Parker (1995) 'The military revolution in seventeenth-century Ireland', pp. 68–88 in J. Ohlmeyer, *Ireland from Independence to Occupation, 1641–1660*, Cambridge.

Lotz-Heumann, U. (2005) 'Confessionalism in Ireland: periodisation and character, 1534–1649', pp. 24–53 in A. Ford and J. McCafferty, *The Origins of Sectarianism in Early Modern Ireland*, Cambridge.

MacCarthy-Morrogh, M. (1986) *The Munster Plantation*, Oxford.

MacLysaght, E. (1939) *Irish Life in the Seventeenth Century*, Dublin, repr. 1979.

Maley, W. (1997) *Salvaging Spenser: Colonialism, Culture and Identity*, London.

Manning, C. (1987) 'A Sheila-na-Gig from Glanworth Castle, Co. Cork', pp. 78–82 in E. Rynne and H. M. Roe, *Figures from the Past*, Dun Loaghaire.

—— (1999) *Clough Outer: A Midlands Castle in Co. Cavan*, Bray.

Markham, G. (1613) *The English Husbandman*, London, repr. 1982.

McCormack, A. M. (2004) 'The social and economic consequences of the Desmond rebellion of 1579–83', *Irish Hist. Studies* 43 No. 133, pp. 1–15.

McCullough, N. and V. Mulvin (1987) *A Lost Tradition: The Nature of Architecture in Ireland*, Dublin, repr. 1989.

McNeill, T. (1997) *Castles in Ireland: Feudal Power in a Gaelic World*, London and New York.

Mallory, J. P. and T. E. McNeill (1982) *The Archaeology of Ulster from Colonization to Plantation,* The Institute of Irish Studies, Queen's University, Belfast.

Moody, T. W. (1937) *The Londonderrry Plantation,* Belfast.

Moody, T. W., F. X. Martin, and F. J. Byrne (1976) *A New History of Ireland,* Oxford.

Morgan, H. (2004), *The Battle of Kinsale,* Bray.

Morton, G. (1971) *Elizabethan Ireland,* London.

Moryson, F. (1617) *An Itinerary,* London.

Mowl, T. (1993) *Elizabethan and Jacobean Style,* London.

Nash, R. C. (1985) 'Irish Atlantic trade in the seventeenth and eighteenth centuries', *William and Mary Quarterly,* 3rd ser., 42, pp. 329–56.

Nicholls, K. (1967) 'Gaelic society and economy in the High Middle Ages', pp. 397–438 in T. W. Moody *et al., Medieval Ireland,* vol. 2, *A New History of Ireland,* Oxford.

Nöel Hume, I. and A. Nöel Hume (2001) *The Archaeology of Martin's Hundred* (Philadelphia and Wiliamsburg.

Norton, R. (1628) *The ... Practise of Artillerie,* London.

O'Danachair, C. (1969) 'Representations of houses on some Irish maps of c. 1600', pp. 91–103 in G. Jenkins, *Studies in Folk Life. Essays in Honour of Iowert C. Peate,* London.

—— (1975) *Ireland's Vernacular Architecture,* Cork.

O'Keeffe, T. (2000) 'Castle-building and the construction of identity: contesting narratives about medieval Ireland', *Irish Geography* 33, pp. 69–88.

—— (2004) 'Barryscourt Castle and the Irish tower-house', pp. 1–32 in J. Ludlow and N. Jameson, *Medieval Ireland: The Barryscourt Lectures I-X,* Kinsale.

—— (2007) 'Plantation-era great houses in Munster: a note on Sir Walter Raleigh's house and its context' pp. 274–89 in T. Herron and M. Potterton, *Ireland in the Renaissance,* Dublin.

Oman, C. (1926) *Castles,* London; repr. New York, 1978.

O'Neil, B. H. St. J. (1960) *Castle and Cannon: A Study of Early Artillery Fortifications in England,* Oxford.

Orpen, G. H. (1903) 'Raleigh's house, Youghal', *J. Royal Soc. of Antiquaries of Ireland* 33, pp. 310–12.

Payne, R. (1589) *Brief Description of Ireland,* London.

Platt, C. (1994) *The Great Buildings of Tudor and Stuart England: Revolutions in Architectural Taste,* London.

Pope Hennessy, J. (1883) *Sir Walter Ralegh in Ireland,* London.

Power, D. (1991) 'The archaeology of the Munster Plantation', pp. 197–201 in M. Ryan, *The Illustrated Archaeology of Ireland,* Dublin.

Priestly, E. J. (1984) 'An early 17th century map of Baltimore', *J. Cork Hist. and Archaeol. Soc.* 89, pp. 55–7.

Quinn, D. B. (1940) *The Voyages and Colonizing Enterprises of Sir Humphrey Gilbert,* London.

—— (1944) 'Sir Thomas Smith (1513–1577) and the beginnings of English colonial theory', *Proceedings of the American Philosophical Society* 88, pp. 543–60.

—— (1947) *Ralegh and the British Empire* (Harmondsworth, repr. 1973).

—— (1958) 'Ireland and sixteenth century European expansion', *Irish Hist. Studies* 11, pp. 20–32.

—— (1964) *Elizabethans and the Irish*, Ithaca, NY.

—— (1966) 'The Munster Plantation: problems and opportunities', *J. Cork Hist. and Archaeol. Soc.* 71, pp. 19–40.

—— (1985) *Set Fair for Roanoke: Voyages and Colonies 1584–1606*, Chapel Hill and London.

Quinn, D. B. and A. M. Quinn (1983) *The New England Voyages 1602–1608*, London.

Ranger, T. O. (1957) 'Richard Boyle and the making of an Irish fortune, 1588–1614', *Irish Hist. Studies* 10, No. 39, pp. 257–97.

Renn, D. (1991) *Kenilworth Castle*, London.

Reps, J. (1972) *Tidewater Towns: City Planning in Colonial Virginia and Maryland*, Williamsburg.

Robinson, P. (1979) 'Vernacular housing in Ulster in the seventeenth century', *Ulster Folklife* 25, pp. 1–28.

—— (1983) '"English" houses built at Moneymore, County Londonderry, *c.* 1615', *Post-Medieval Archaeol.* 17, pp. 47–64.

Ronnes, H. (2007) 'Continental traces at Carrick-on-Suir and contemporary Irish castles: a preliminary study of date-and-initial stones', pp. 255–73 in T. Herron and M. Potterton, *Ireland in the Renaissance*, Dublin.

Rowse, A. L. (1955) *The Expansion of Elizabethan England*, London.

—— (1971) *The Elizabethan Renaissance: The Cultural Achievement*, Chicago.

Ryan, M. (1991) *The Illustrated Archaeology of Ireland*, Dublin.

Salter, M. (1993) *Castles and Stronghouses of Ireland*, Malvern.

Salzman, L. F. (1952) *Building in England Down to 1546: A Documentary History*, Oxford.

Sheehan, A. J. (1982) 'The population of the plantation of Munster: Quinn reconsidered', *J. Cork Hist. and Archaeol. Soc.* 87, pp. 107–17.

—— (1983) 'The overthrow of the Munster Plantation', *Irish Sword* 15 (1982–83), pp. 11–22.

Silke, J. (1970) *Kinsale: The Spanish Intervention in Ireland at the End of the Elizabethan Wars*, New York.

Stafford, T. (1633) *Pacata Hibernia*, London.

Strong, R. C. (1979) *The Renaissance Garden in England*, London.

Summerson, J. (1982) 'The defense of the realm under Elizabeth I', pp. 402–14 in H. M. Colvin, *History of the King's Works Vol. IV 1485–1660 (Part II)*, London.

Swift, M. (1999) *Historical Maps of Ireland*, London.

Thompson, M. W. (1987) *The Decline of the Castle*, Cambridge.

Townshend, D. (1904) *The Life and Letters of the Great Earl of Cork*, London.

Toy, S. (1955) *A History of Fortification*, London.

Trevelyan, R. (2002) *Sir Walter Raleigh*, London and New York, 2004.

Waterman, D. M. (1961) 'Some Irish seventeenth-century houses and their architectural ancestry', pp. 251–74, in E. M. Jope (ed.), *Studies in Building History. Essays dedicated to B. H. St J. O'Neil*, London.

Webb, H. J. (1965) *Elizabethan Military Science. The Books and the Practice*, Madison, Wisconsin.

Wood, M. (1965) *The English Medieval House*, London.

Index

Note: Because the textual divisions of chapters and subchapters are by topic, the Table of Contents provides the reader with a guide to particular themes.